THE SOUL OF A DOG

DESTRUCTURING BEHAVIOR AND THE CONSTRUCT OF CONSCIOUSNESS

JAMES TSAI

THE LUXURY OF CONSCIOUSNESS

How to support my work in saving innocent dysfunctional dogs from the ineptitude of "behavioral euthanasia" by buying a copy for your friends

Visit www.TheSoulOfaDog.com

All familial-species enjoy the luxury of consciousness.

Dedication

My surrogate children: Lincoln Tsai, Nero Tsai, Sammie Tsai, Walter Tsai, Lincoln Tsai Jr., Mingki Tsai, William Tsai, David Tsai, Stephen Tyrion Tsai, Jonathan Tsai, Maple Tsai, Rosie Tsai, and Andrew Hugo Tsai.

Leaders Press, for without CEO Alinka Rutkowska's brilliant prescience, my work would've been lost.

Table of Contents

Foreword

I was first introduced to James several years ago through my volunteer work with a dog rescue group in Vancouver, BC. I was intrigued by his work. As I delved deeper into it, I realized it was not only unique but also profoundly effective.

In my personal experience with James, I had a little rescue dog that was having aggression issues. I sought guidance from all of my professional trainer friends, along with everything I could find online. All ended up ineffective to help with her aggressions toward some of my other dogs. I then consulted with Arf Arf Bark Bark Rescue Foundation and, by following James's methodology, was able to resolve most of her problems and allowed for easily managing the miniscule quirks that remained.

Upon getting another rescue dog who had extreme fear aggression, I began using these techniques–or might I say life insights–immediately, and they made a world of difference. I truly believe he would still be biting if it were not for this training.

I have since gotten a third rescue dog, one lacking proper cognition of socialization, and I am utilizing similar abilities to integrate his interactions with our other dogs. I would never have been able to do these things without James's skills and knowledge, as well as his willingness to want to help every dog he can.

While doing training classes myself, I have always believed in having many tools to utilize in my dog-training tool belt–and I still do, but those are now reserved for training skills, not so much for addressing behavior anymore.

It is, to a degree, understandable that the training community at large wants to put down the viscerally intuitive dog training he presents. I believe it is because they think that someone without a degree or professional training is incapable of such amazingly adaptive theory. One does not need those things to be an astute observer of behavior. It becomes obvious he has spent many years watching, learning, and refining this modality into its current remarkable form.

And what greater testament is there than downtraining a predatory dog–one who had attacked and even tried to kill people–into a solid, stable dog in the home?

Do trainers think they will lose out on their livelihood? In reality, they are actually gaining incredible methods to assist them. Think of it this way: by getting on board with this training, I believe there will be many more dogs saved and many more people will be able to manage their dogs– bringing their dogs out of a bad state and into a proper family orientation where all enjoy life, human and canine alike.

How many dogs are euthanized monthly simply because they display fear- or aggression-based issues–issues that are often minor, sometimes major, yet ultimately correctable? Sadly, usually caused by humans. If shelters began to implement this training, more dogs would have a chance to live instead of losing their life.

I am continually learning what this training strategy has to offer and plan to become more proficient, along with the hope that many more will follow and discover that James is light years ahead of the pack. I hope I have the chance to pick up even half of what he knows. It can be brain challenging, but quite simple too.

Just open up to your intuitive side!

Yvette O'Connor

Expawmation Animal Rehabilitation Therapy

Charter Member of Moore United Animal Therapy Association; Dog Trainer at Obedience Training Club of Chugiak; Dog Rescue Volunteer; Animal Sports enthusiast, Former Sprint Musher, Animal Lover

Preface

The Soul of a Dog: Destructuring Behavior and the Construct of Consciousness brings forth the Arf Arf Bark Bark Theorem of Consciousness and of Learning. Its disaggregation and destructure resulted from the uniqueness of over 30,000 hours working with human and animal predatory, extremely vicious dogs weighing between 150 to 211 pounds, with shoulders (withers) measuring thirty-eight inches. This work was conducted alone inside my home–free-range, unmuzzled, and without personal protection. At times, there were as many as eight dogs in a familial setting, each epitomizing profound psychological complexity that exceeds the aggregate knowledge of the world's universities, behavior and zoology experts, and far beyond the world's top master dog trainers.

The theorem's empirical comprehension spans the behaviorism spectrum–from normal through to profound extreme dysfunctions–which manifest chronically in the most commonly domesticated species: dogs. As the world's only expert, my book reflects the accurate comprehension of behavior and quantifying consciousness in dogs, as well as how their psychology correlates within all familial-species. Ironically, this debunks the tired academic mantra "evidence-based results" as nothing more than anthropomorphized inexperience.

My work directly scales human to animal behavior relative to the evolutional construct of consciousness.

Dog experts **must** rehabilitate all dogs, regardless of the complexity of dysfunction.

Dog experts **never** condone *behavioral euthanasia.*

Dog experts **never** use food, brute force, alpha/leader, prong, e-collar, shock, or slip collars.

Dog experts **never** condone medication for dysfunctional behavior.

The Soul of a Dog: Destructuring Behavior and the Construct of Consciousness (by Arf Arf Bark Bark Rescue Foundation) introduces the world's only empirically-proven cure for *behavioral euthanasia* and the first logical phylogenesis of consciousness inter alia behavior–accurate, non-speculative comprehension, backed by proof of the theorem. It will also advance artificial intelligence toward attaining the Artificial Contextual Intelligence necessary for artificial consciousness.

I stand vehemently against efforts to commercialize or bastardize my work or my life without my legally contracted endorsement. This effectively denounces any efforts after my death unless pre-contracted.

There are **NO** individuals, dog trainers, organizations, or corporations affiliated with Arf Arf Bark Bark Rescue Foundation or with me, either in the past or present. Other than Yvette, I have not trained or certified anyone in the direct or indirect industry, nor have I worked with any accreditation faculty or academia. From these same corners, I have only experienced apathy, indifference, and personal attacks.

Behaviorism, its academia, PPAB, IAABC, CAPDT, CCPDT, and others would have remained blissfully medieval in wantonly deeming dangerous, skittish, and predatory dogs as deserving of being killed. At my proficiency, self-deluded "dog aggression experts" would be killed within minutes and their bodies eviscerated thereafter–yet they audaciously self-aggrandize, spreading their virulent miscomprehension and shallow visceral empathy through *behavioral euthanasia*.

My work falsifies Karl Popper's falsification opine, as shown in my YouTube and social media videos, in which every dog profoundly exceeds the aggregate knowledge of behaviorism academe's so-called "modern science" and "evidence-based" bunk. My work doesn't challenge the industry; it completely destroys it.

In closing, the imperative for federal licensing of any persons breeding dogs, whether accidental or deliberate, requires political empathy and judicial maturation. The domestication of dogs and cats is **not** a human right; it is a privilege.

Acknowledgments

God, for sharing a gift with me.

Part 1
Who Am I?

Introduction

My family left China in the early 1960s, embarking on a transformative journey that led to our legal emigration to Canada. We established our North American chapter in Vancouver and later relocated to the picturesque city of Victoria. In the grand tapestry, I occupy the sixth position among eight siblings—an arrangement beautifully alternating between four girls and four boys. I hold the distinction of being the firstborn outside China.

From a young age, I possessed an innate sense of self-awareness. My mind was a canvas upon which I painted deliberate "memories," thoughts, and emotions, all with the intention of revisiting them in my forties and fifties. This early practice laid the foundation for my enduring fascination with the boundless potential of consciousness.

Our life in Victoria was intertwined with the presence of our uncle, a prominent ophthalmologist. Given the relative scarcity of the Chinese community in Victoria, people often mistook him for our father. This created a subtle backdrop of expectations regarding success, perpetuated by our parents' dreams that all their children would achieve financial prosperity.

Intelligence ran deep in our family's DNA. My eldest brother, David, was a mathematical prodigy, pursuing double minors in math at the University of Victoria. On the other end, my youngest brother, Daniel (with an astounding IQ of 166), embarked on a brilliant legal career and, assisted by our parents bequeathing him millions of dollars in property, comfortably retired in his early forties. Today, Daniel imparts his legal wisdom as a professor, prolific columnist, advisor, and partner with businesses in China.[1]

David, with an IQ of 152, held a pivotal position as the sole technical lead on Sun Microsystems Canada's national sales team in the early 2000s, handling contracts of eight-figure magnitude.

[1] Daniel Tsai, "Daniel Tsai: Freelance Columnist at The Toronto Star," Muck Rack, accessed September 16, 2025, https://muckrack.com/daniel-tsai

As I approached the age of ten, I found myself irresistibly drawn into the intricate world of chess. Surprisingly, I managed to achieve a remarkable feat—winning against David in chess approximately thirty percent of the time. Recognizing my potential, my father intervened, advocating for my acceleration in school. By the time I reached grade 5, I was delving into algebra, and by grade 6, I had ventured into the realm of calculus.

Our dad, a professor in China, spoke seventeen languages fluently and could recite a wide swath of academia and factual history. Our mom grew up without formal education, yet her photographic memory and ability to contextualize significant information made her a formidable inspiration.

Music also played a significant role in my life, offering a glimpse into my potential as a pianist. At the tender age of ten, I had the opportunity to attend the Royal Victoria Conservatory for Music. Sadly, my parents' stern approach and stringent expectations essentially extinguished my passion for music.

My formal education, despite its promise, eventually fell short of my evolving consciousness. In eighth-grade computer science, I was already programming my own version of Pac-Man in BASIC—this was circa 1981, when we shared communal five-inch floppy disk drives. By grade 10, I had grown bored, which led to my decision to discontinue my academic pursuits. The curriculum felt detached from practicality and relevance, leaving me disillusioned. My growing consciousness led me to conclude that the traditional education system couldn't adequately nourish my intellect. I did attempt to complete grade 12 at another high school. Still, the disconnect between my aspirations and the educational landscape persisted.

While a career in law beckoned as a tempting prospect, I couldn't ignore the shadow it cast on my inherent personality. My ability to decipher the intricacies of human psychology and dissect complex issues would have propelled me to prioritize financial success and brutally accumulate victories. The broader, global perspective I held could have been eclipsed by a relentless pursuit of material wealth.

Amidst my journey of introspection, I dedicated considerable time to contemplation. Our family's early struggles meant limited social connections, and I often found myself alone in deep thought. Our modest means translated into frugality, with each school year marked by a mere two sets of clothing, a testament to my mother's resourcefulness during those trying times.

Yet, beneath the surface of my contemplative existence lay a darker truth. My second oldest brother, Joseph, harbored a deeply troubling darkness within him. He subjected my younger sister, Betty, to a harrowing ordeal of abuse. I remained blissfully unaware for years, listening in silent anguish to the horrors unfolding behind the locked door of his bedroom.

Joseph's cruelty didn't end with Betty; it extended to me as well. I recall two consecutive summers when he subjected me to brutal physical abuse—wielding a baseball bat to strike my knees and subjecting me to relentless beatings until I was left hyperventilating. In my early forties, I summoned the courage to contact the Victoria Police multiple times, seeking justice for the abuse I endured. My efforts were met with disheartening apathy, a painful reminder of the injustices that persist in Victoria.

One of my earliest memories was of the huge fights my parents would have with our oldest sister, Rose. She was only thirteen at the time, and her boyfriend, Donald Robertson, was twenty-four years old. Donald refused to respect my parents' orders to leave their prepubescent daughter alone. Donald immigrated from New Zealand to escape criminal assault charges and clearly didn't "turn a new leaf." Rose would sneak out at night to spend time with Donald in his apartment. Her grades cratered. She was in the seventh grade at the time. My parents phoned the Victoria Police numerous times, but they took no action regarding Donald. Donald convinced Rose to run away with him after turning fourteen. Donald waited until she was old enough to legally marry her. Worse, my niece and nephew, Channel and Jeremy, are children of a pedophile, and they carry intense hatred of their father.

My first foray into the world of employment was at the golden arches of McDonald's. The journey to secure this position was not without its stumbles. I vividly recall my first interview, where the manager posed the quintessential question about my future goals at McDonald's. My response was perhaps overzealous; I aspired to eventually take over the manager's role. Alas, the position eluded me that day. My older siblings all worked at McDonald's and achieved promotions to assistant manager and manager.

Undeterred, I turned my sights to the downtown Victoria location of McDonald's, where I wisely refrained from declaring my managerial ambitions. At seventeen years old, I joined the ranks as a full-time employee, diligently contributing to the bustling lunch-hour service, earning $2.35 per hour. My performance consistently ranked among the highest during these busy hours.

Opportunity knocked when a position materialized for a maintenance worker on the night shift. Eager to advance, I approached the manager with a proposal to work double shifts, all without expecting overtime compensation. I endured this grueling schedule for approximately five months until it dawned on me that this tireless dedication wouldn't yield the advancement I sought. It was then that I chose to part ways with McDonald's and explore new horizons.

Soon, I found myself navigating the challenging terrain of holding down three jobs concurrently. By day, I stocked supermarket shelves. When night fell, I donned the role of a nightclub bouncer. My nights didn't end; they continued as I transitioned to a janitorial role at the pub upstairs, owned by the same proprietor. This relentless pursuit of multiple employment was, in part, my way of striving to meet my parents' expectations.

However, life had its share of challenges. I encountered legal troubles related to driving with a suspended license, primarily attributed to my youthful escapades on a motorcycle. At that time, the consequences for driving under such circumstances included mandatory jail time, a policy later challenged and overturned by the Supreme Court of Canada for violating constitutional rights.

My marriage was marked by its own set of trials. A deep-seated shyness, stemming from my school years, colored my early adult life. I remained a virgin into my early twenties, and my perceptions of love and relationships were heavily influenced by television shows like *Leave It to Beaver*, even though they aired before my time. I recall huddling around our little black-and-white TV with extended antenna wires, absorbing the idealized portrayal of family life.

However, my life took a different trajectory after I got married. My spouse, who had initially worked as a McDonald's manager, arbitrarily withdrew from the workforce, leaving me to shoulder the responsibility of Hypatia Shoes, a unique shoe store venture. While I toiled at the store, she chose to remain at home and declined to assist with its operations.

I worked to expand the business into related markets and communities. By the end of the first year, the store was consistently grossing $30,000 monthly. I purchased the factory of one of my suppliers, Sunset Strip Shoes, and split my time in Van Nuys, California. I advertised in the popular free weekly *Georgia Straight* and on NEWS1130 radio.

I started an athletic wear clothing line through the store, branding it Define Athletics. I fitted the BC Lions cheerleaders for Alexandra Severyn*, Felions Dance Manager, with athletic yoga wear in the late 2000s. I hired a draftsperson who was later hired as manager for Lululemon's East Asia division.

Our marriage was tumultuous, marred by physical altercations that led to both of us facing charges of spousal assault during our early years of marriage. The burden of supporting our family rested squarely on my shoulders as she adamantly resisted employment. This pattern repeated itself in every entrepreneurial endeavor I undertook, with me as the sole breadwinner, often following heated disagreements.

JETSAI SuperCar Transport[2] mirrored this pattern with her continued reluctance to contribute, manage paperwork, or provide assistance. She nevertheless enjoyed the new SUVs every six months and a $25,000 credit card limit. I eventually learned she was having multiple extracurricular relationships. The strain took a toll on my mental well-being as I worked twenty-one-hour days for weeks in a row. Over the course of ten years, JETSAI transported $1 billion in supercars.

Amidst these challenges, I found solace and expression in the world of entertainment. I pursued acting and stand-up comedy for many years.[3] Stand-up comedy became my medium of choice, offering an avenue for my creativity to flourish. This shared emotional experience, akin to the rush of delivering a humorous joke on stage or witnessing a singer move an entire audience, became a significant part of my life's tapestry.

---

* https://www.bclions.com/2021/03/08/international-womens-day-lions-impact/

2 JETSAI SuperCar Transport is a high-value, specialized vehicle transportation carrier. For more information, search JETSAI Specialized SuperCar Transport on Facebook.

3 James Tsai, IMDb, accessed September 16, 2025, https://www.imdb.com/name/nm1526297/

CHAPTER 1

A Glimpse Into *The Soul of a Dog*

In *The Soul of a Dog*, I want to embark on a transformative journey that delves deep into the realm of dog behavior, consciousness, and the intricate bond between humans and animals. I wish to leave behind a heartfelt plea to reshape academia's understanding of consciousness across all forms of life. By doing so, I believe we can revolutionize the way we interpret behavior and elevate our comprehension to new heights.

Through a blend of personal experiences and meticulous exploration, I hope the book shines a light on the profound miscomprehensions hindering our societal evolution, holding back our potential progress in various realms, including human advancement and technological breakthroughs. Within the core of this narrative lies a passionate drive to redefine our understanding of behaviorism and consciousness. I debunk all existing dog-training methodologies, exposing their significant inadequacies and advocating for a paradigm shift in our interactions. Throughout these pages, I'll guide readers through a process of dissecting complex behaviors into manageable fragments, fostering a stronger connection between human consciousness and animal consciousness. In turn, the book destroys the practice of *behavioral euthanasia* as systemic ineptitude, empirically disproving that extremely dangerous, predatory, or highly skittish dogs must be killed.

The Soul of a Dog: Destructuring Behavior and the Construct of Consciousness is intentionally written with neologisms. Instead of "conscious," animals possess "consciousness" and behave "consciousnessly," in order to provide scale of behavior. With "specie" as singular, we're not defaulting as human exclusivity when discussing *familial-species behaving consciousnessly.*

Hyphenations are intentional: "familial-species," "familial-specie," "reset-hug."

The unfolding narrative weaves a compelling tale of interconnected destinies among dogs, humans, and familial-species. It explores the impact of our perceptions of behavior on the relationships we form, delving into themes of egocentrism, egoselfishness, intradependency, codependency, and the inherently primal instincts binding us since the beginning of evolution.

This book underscores the significance of embracing intuition—and yes, of intuitively anthropomorphizing behavior—to enhance the deep bonds we share cohabitatively.

My central message is the urgent need to revolutionize academic paradigms. I call for a comprehensive reevaluation of conventional dog training approaches, stressing the potency of understanding and empathetic communication over punitive and transactive measures. I unwaveringly prove an empirically effective and real alternative to *behavioral euthanasia*: rehabilitation for all dysfunctional behaviors—regardless of breed, genetics, age, or gender, intact or not—is fully possible.

Consciousness creates behavior, and behavior creates consciousness.

Ultimately, *The Soul of a Dog* is an offering of hope and empowerment to dog parents. It reassures them that even the most complex and challenging behaviors in their beloved companions can be rectified through a profoundly accurate comprehension of behavior and consciousness. By unraveling the intricate layers of dog behavior and psychology, the book aims to cultivate harmony within families and among different species, encouraging readers to adopt a fresh perspective that reshapes their relationships with dogs, elevates their overall quality of life, and promotes a stronger sense of intelligence.

I never envisioned my life story to be the first book I'd write nor did I intend to be the author of a narrative that delves into my personal journey. My initial plans did not include this. I was aware of the difficulty separating "James Tsai" from "'James Tsai's work"—particularly unravelling one of the most complex enigmas known to humanity: consciousness.

My journey has been one of complex revelations, a path marked by an unmatched dedication to understanding, empathy, and advocacy. At its heart, my work seeks to address a deeply troubling issue: *behavioral euthanasia*, which is preventable and rehabilitable. This is the root of my life's work. It's become much more than a reliable refrain; it's an unavoidable indictment of professional and academic malpractice. Dogs are the most common domesticated specie living with humans. North Americans have 110 million domesticated dogs; many of these dogs exhibit dysfunctional behaviors.

Attacking, biting, fighting, destruction, protecting assets, OCD, and agoraphobia/skittishness exist in all dogs. All dogs are born predators. Parents of dysfunctional dogs describe negative and antisocial behaviors that are common everywhere in the world. Behavior is psychologically homogenous across the entire taxa of *domesticable Canis familiaris*. The commonness of dysfunctions further proves behavior is NOT "breed-specific" and NOT genetic-preponderant.

I began to realize the profound implications of my findings. The gravity of the situation dawned on me–six million dysfunctional dogs meet a tragic end each year due to collective academic failure. This failure has far-reaching consequences, including a distorted understanding of the very foundation of human behavior.

I know my work extends beyond the realms of conventional academia, surpassing the limitations of past theories and researchers, such as B.F. Skinner. It's not an easy position to be in. Academic institutions, with their established norms, accepted dogmas, and incentivized educational grants, seldom entertain autodidactic work due to egotistical-regressive demands for credentialed education. My initial attempts to engage with academia were met with indifference and often outright profane dismissal.

I've always been aware of the challenge of gaining recognition from the academic world. My quest isn't driven by a desire for personal glory; it's about saving the lives of countless animals. Dogs, cats, horses, cows, sheep, and chickens–they all deserve better. My work holds the key to transforming their lives and maturing jurisprudence.

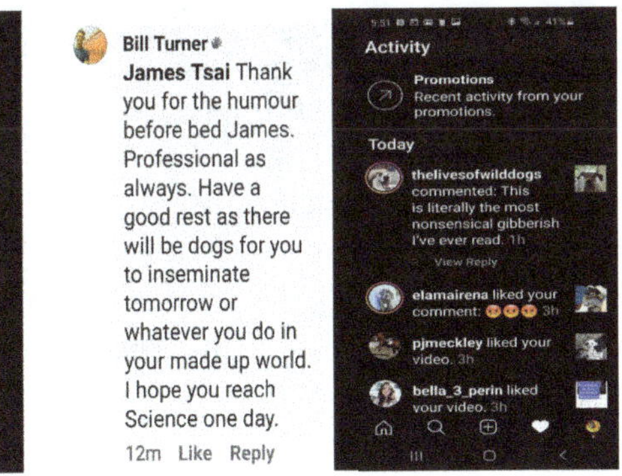

The relentless stream of antipathy and derision of my work has existed from day one through to present day.

Academia, despite its vast resources and knowledge, consistently fails to grasp the fundamentals of behavior and consciousness. Blindly following what's considered authoritative, even when it's demonstrably wrong. *Modern science*, as it stands, has never come close to unraveling the true depths of consciousness.

My work offers a comprehensive understanding of consciousness. It presents a plausible theory backed by undeniable evidence. It's not about besting Darwin; it's about standing on the shoulders of giants to see further. My work can change the course of history, but it's met with resistance, skepticism, and even hostility.

Before I thought of writing the book, I'd spent 30,000 hours working with dogs refused by the "best minds" in America. They knew they were witlessly outmatched when confronted with human predation. Critics may question my qualifications, but my success rate remains at 100 percent across the entire spectrum of dysfunctions, without exception. "Any dog, any severity of dysfunction, in real time." All with only a basic collar and a basic leash. Critics couldn't face the same frightening challenges.

The academic world is insular and arrogant, entrenched in its classical beliefs, and refusing to acknowledge the failures of its own "evidence-based" systems, instead perpetuating the status quo. My work devastates its entire framework, and I'm not willing to compromise its integrity for the sake of academic recognition.

My book isn't aimed at the ivory towers of academia; it's for the tens of millions of dog parents. They are the audience that matters. Dog owners spend $14 billion annually on pet care, including training, the most expensive non-medical expense for them. My work significantly reduces these costs while enhancing the lives of dogs and their human parents.

As I navigate the tumultuous waters of academic indifference, I'm grateful for the opportunity to share my personal findings on behaviorism. As I've shared, my goal isn't personal glory; it's to ensure that my work reaches the masses and saves countless lives in the process. Whether academia acknowledges it or not, my theorem is here to stay, challenging convention and transforming our understanding.

Above all, this book aspires to ignite a transformative paradigm shift. I invite readers to recognize that human evolution is rooted in a profound understanding of behavior, consciousness, and the intricate connections we share with the diverse species that inhabit the planet. Please join me on a journey that promises to not only redefine our perceptions of our beloved canine companions but also deepen our understanding of ourselves–and the very essence of life itself.

CHAPTER 2

A Personal Odyssey with Dogs

My journey has been a series of unexpected twists and turns, leading me from the world of stand-up comedy to an extraordinary connection with animals, particularly dogs. This shift, transitioning from comedy to a more profound calling, was driven by my desire to evoke emotional resonance akin to the impact of a captivating show or a perfectly timed joke. I came to realize that just as singers move their audiences, animals touch our hearts with self-awareness.

This evolution has been marked by my profound relationship with dogs, a relationship that mirrors my personal growth. Despite my childhood fear of public performance, which ironically steered me towards comedy, it was my experiences with animals that unveiled my true passion. Among all animals, dogs played an exceptional role in reshaping the trajectory of my life. However, this profound connection wasn't forged without its challenges.

During my childhood, I was haunted by a traumatic encounter with a German Shepherd. This fear lingered well into my early adulthood, rendering even friendly dogs seemingly threatening. As a child, my near-drowning experience and being resuscitated added layers of trauma that colored my interactions with the world.

Despite these formidable fears, my journey led me to develop a deep connection with the world of animals, especially dogs, in a way that resonated deeply. I chose to adopt dogs with human predation, defying prevalent notions of their "hopelessness." This journey was characterized by my inherent talent to identify and comprehend psychosomatic manifestations of their psychological dysfunction and emotive complexity.

The loss of both my parents, who served as mentors and guiding lights, thrust me into navigating this unconventional path solo. Their absence remains palpable as I navigate this path, dedicated to my passion and my dogs, even in the face of financial challenges.

My early interactions, particularly with Lincoln, Nero, Walter, Lincoln Jr., William, and David, embody my life-risking commitment to successfully rehabilitating giant dogs with profoundly troubled histories. These experiences propelled me into developing Parenting Protocols that accurately describe dog behavior psychology. My interactions with Nero and Walter, the most challenging at the time, were beautifully profound lessons about the depths of true love, loyal trust, and painful grief, respectively.

Lincoln Tsai

After my marriage dissolved into divorce, I wanted to sell the house, but my ex refused. Years of apathy for our businesses, coupled with her extramarital affairs, had emboldened her. What disturbed me most was her $250,000 ICBC insurance fraud, all while she actively worked for JETSAI. But her apathy for our disabled daughter was the last straw.

Our daughter, diagnosed with spastic diplegia cerebral palsy, was constantly bullied at Erma Stephenson Elementary School, despite the regional supervision of Theresa Campbell[4]—who ironically had headed the district's *Safer School* program. Between grades 5 and 7, the bullying escalated until my daughter began openly talking about killing herself. This was inexplicable to me.

One circumstance occurred when I was at my shoe factory in Van Nuys. Our daughter became angry, grabbed a butcher knife and a five-pound block of cheese from the fridge. She then frantically stabbed the cheese, damaging the countertops. Screaming uncontrollably, she urinated on herself. I was trying to run a new business while worried about her. Her mother, however, refused to confront Erma Stephenson Elementary.[5] I was fighting the walls our family's matriarch deliberately put up and the cynical Safer Schools program, with Theresa caring more about the Caucasian bullies than my suicidal daughter.

I lived in basement suites, then finally, a one-bedroom apartment in a brand-new building that allowed dogs of any size. The woman I was dating had

[4] Theresa Campbell, "Theresa Campbell," Safer Schools Together, accessed September 16, 2025, https://saferschoolstogether.com/our-team/theresa-campbell/

[5] u/rainman_104, "Grade 7 girl with cerebral palsy bullied. School takes no action on the bullying," Reddit, r/canada, November 3, 2010, https://www.reddit.com/r/canada/comments/effud/grade_7_girl_with_cerebral_palsy_bullied_school/

purchased a beautiful female fawn, a Great Dane. I thought about adopting instead. I considered whether I was ready and responsible enough. Would I be committed to my dog for their entire life? Great Danes are three to four times the expense of a fifty-pound dog. Every time we walked, we received unsolicited comments from insensitive strangers, such as, "Great Danes don't live long" to, "Is that a horse?"

When I met Lincoln for the first time, it was after weeks of anticipation. He was middle-aged. After weeks of communication, the family drove from Alberta to Vancouver to surrender him. It was a chilly winter evening on November 5, 2014. Lincoln's immense presence filled my small one-bedroom apartment—some family members even had to sit on the floor. Lincoln weighed 154 pounds, a giant both in stature and spirit, and came from a line of Canadian grand champions by Rachel Crozier.

Lincoln would become a unique and remarkable companion in my life's journey. At five and a half years old, his family faced significant challenges in handling his behavior around other dogs, leading them to place him in boarding facilities for periods of six months or more. However, such facilities often employ techniques that can be detrimental to dogs with underlying dysfunctions, relying on force, coercion, and dominance-based methods that can't address core dysfunctions.

My journey with Lincoln began. One of Lincoln's prominent challenges was his intense interest in prey. At just four months old, Lincoln captured and killed a baby squirrel. Notably, he guarded the lifeless body for a substantial 45 minutes before his family could retrieve the squirrel. I was inexperienced, and our education together began. It was clear from the start that Lincoln had a complex past, one filled with neglect and misunderstandings. He'd never felt the cohesiveness of family. The first few weeks were challenging. Lincoln was anxious, unsure of his new surroundings, and carrying the emotional scars of his past. He would display destructive behaviors, tearing through furniture and barking relentlessly when I left for work. But I refused to give up on him.

Lincoln began my first step toward developing my own principles of the theorem of consciousness and learning. Instead of trying to dominate Lincoln or force obedience, it was a journey of patience, compassion, and understanding. I began to develop communication and language structures that follow the evolutionary structure of human communication. As days turned into weeks, Lincoln began to change. His anxiety lessened, and he started to trust me. Our bond grew stronger with every passing day. I communicated with Lincoln using nonverbal cues and observed the tiniest of his responses, learning to understand his needs and emotions directly correlated with how Lincoln consequently behaved in response. Lincoln stopped lunging at other dogs. He stopped barking at other dogs. People who had known Lincoln with his previous family would remark that Lincoln was a completely different, calmer dog than before. I didn't take such comments as a compliment on my efforts, as I was saddened that Lincoln had suffered psychologically most of his life.

Over time, Lincoln transformed. His destructive behaviors disappeared, replaced by a calm and loving demeanor. He became a source of inspiration for my work, a living testament to the power of understanding and compassion, not the brutality of coercive devices or the use of food to bribe compliance. Dogs and animals comprehend familialship.

It was a matter of proving to Lincoln that I'd protect him as his parent when he saw other dogs. Lincoln's anger was actually rooted in not feeling protected, reminding him of being attacked in boarding. He stabilizes and calmed more quickly when I brought him close to me and held him in what I'd refined as the *reset-hug*. This helped Lincoln feel physically safe from danger.

I overcame my caution, giving him reset-hugs when Lincoln was upset. The more I held Lincoln in a consistent, firm reset-hug, he'd calm down slightly sooner in each circumstance. It made sense to provide Lincoln with the same thing a human child expects from its parents: protection.

We occasionally welcomed other dogs into our home as fosters. One such case was Melody, a fifty-pound Great Dane mix from Taiwan. Her rescue reached out to me for assistance, hearing of my success with Lincoln. Melody came with her set of challenges, including extreme skittishness, biting people, and zero recall. Her rescue had already invested over $1,500 in training that proved ineffective.

Melody's first week with me showed remarkable progress; she quickly learned recall without using treats and began approaching people for affection. Her rescue was very impressed. This further reinforced my belief that healing and stabilizing each dog occurs when we provide a safe emotional harbor. Our journey together was not without challenges, but it was a journey of profound growth and transformation–for both of us. Lincoln had taught me that every dog, no matter their past, possesses a sophisticated consciousness that deserves to be acknowledged and nurtured. Melody was no different.

Sadly, our time together was cut short. After six months, Lincoln developed a limp and had trouble walking on his rear right leg. Fearing cancer, it turned out to be an extremely aggressive bacterial infection. As it spread, Lincoln became paraplegic. I bought him a Great Dane-sized wheelchair. Within four weeks, Lincoln became incontinent, generating multiple loads of laundry daily.

On New Year's Day, I brought Lincoln in for a routine status check. X-rays showed clear lungs. In sixteen days, I was saying Goodbye to my beloved puppy boy at the emergency hospital due to severe respiratory distress. Lincoln's lungs had become a mass of pneumonia with no hope of recovery. In the end, it wasn't just Lincoln who had been saved–it was I who had undergone a profound change. Being Lincoln's human surrogate parent, the concept of *family* is represented by the protections between child and parent. Lincoln was my surrogate child. I cried when he died.

Each beloved Soul leaves an indelible mark on my heart and enriches my wisdom in their wake. Lincoln, the original patriarch, infused my life with the lesson of grief. His passing introduced me to the pangs of death's embrace. Lincoln's legacy graced my life and radiated a wise awareness of the world. His tragic departure became an introduction. Lincoln underscored connections that transcend the physical realm, teaching me that the bond forged is eternal. I learned to honor and celebrate life, even in the fleeting moments. The pain of losing Lincoln was my first encounter with profound loss. This experience taught me how to cope with grief and navigate the challenges of saying Goodbye to a cherished family member and beloved friend.

Lincoln taught me Loss.

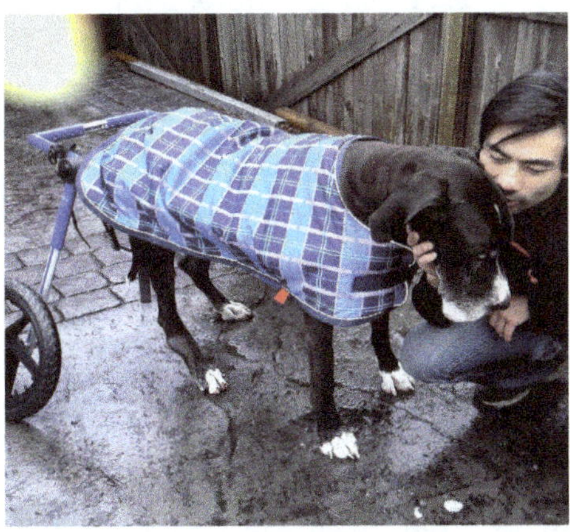

My beloved Lincoln in his final weeks as he went from actively running to paraplegic to dying at emergency from severe respiratory distress.

Nina (rehabilitation)

A pregnant harlequin Great Dane was abandoned. Nina is Melody's mom. The rescue was so impressed with Melody that they asked if I'd rehabilitate her. Nina flew from Taiwan. Nina was found with the Great Dane sire at a light rail construction site, giving birth two days after rescue. Nina had cropped ears and deep scars around her mouth from a thick wire wrapped around her muzzle by an unlicensed backyard breeder. She had been beaten if she defended herself, which left her extremely afraid and very agoraphobic of the outside world.

In Nina's first week with me, she did the impossible: she walked through downtown Vancouver by St. Paul's Hospital, despite the crowd and traffic. I gave Nina sustained reset-hugs often. Nina was afraid of everything—even dropping her own food while eating. She wouldn't eat food in front of me. She was afraid to walk the carpeted hallway of our apartment building or through the parking garage. Nighttime abjectly frightened Nina, with the darkness camouflaging the cars and whizzing headlights. Falling rain immobilized Nina—she froze and couldn't move.

Nina is very gentle and never gets upset. She didn't understand the world because she had lived in the cruel world of the unlicensed backyard breeder. On our nighttime walks, when it rained, Nina immediately became too afraid to walk. She noticeably shook. The distance between the bathroom area and the entrance is 200 feet (sixty meters). I'd crouch alongside Nina and say her name—giving her long sustained reset-hugs each time. Walking the distance took forty-five minutes to the front door. Lincoln, Nina, and I would be drenched in our jackets. Streams of water seeped under my clothes.

Stabilizing Nina required literally habilitating the sophistication of her impaired cogency. Dysfunctions happened circumstantially, so Lincoln and I were giving Nina a beautiful life that she never could have imagined. The foreign familial complexity was very difficult for Nina to psychologically process. Nina stabilized and began to approach strangers with nary hesitation. Nina was adopted by one of the rescue's dog trainers, whom they had previously hired for Melody.

I remember visiting Nina one month after her adoption. She stared at me as if seeing a ghost, never imagining she would see me again. She was elated, wanting to leave with me. That was the last time I ever saw her.

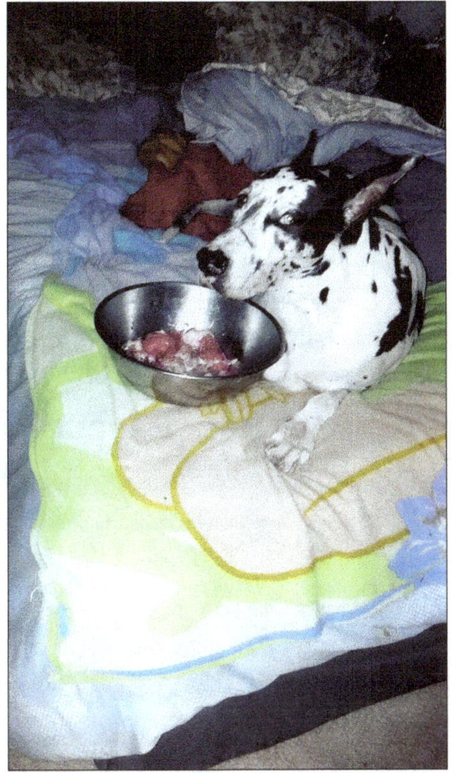

Nina enjoying a nice meal in bed.

Nero Tsai (Negro)

Nero, with a heart as big as his stature, also came from a life of loneliness. After Lincoln's death, I felt I could never adopt again. My heart and body hurt so much losing Lincoln. I knew his life was too important. I needed to pay tribute to Lincoln's legacy. My profound intelligence recognized significant cogency in every dog, so I began searching for a Great Dane as extremely dangerous as possible. Profound viciousness was my minimum requirement–ideally, an extremely predatory senior.

Nero's story is a testament to resilience: a ten-year, four-month-old Great Dane rescued from a dire situation in Alabama. Nero's life was marked by cruelty and hardship. An unlicensed backyard breeder caged him for the first seven years, and he spent the next three years chained outside with a prong collar. Nero's black neckline was encircled by a prominent band of white fur scars. The cruelty of his entire life in Alabama was reflected in his original name: "Negro."

An old dog requires the exact same for fulsome rehabilitation as a young dog.

Nero weighed a mere seventy-five pounds, far below the healthy 140 pounds he should have been. He had been dumped at the kill shelter by his family. It was clear Nero's life had been filled with pain and neglect–a heartbreaking reflection that dogs are judicially regarded as property.

Arf Arf Bark Bark Rescue Foundation

The legal argument for recognizing dogs as Functional Sentient Beings:

A person injured in a MVA can sue for damage to their vehicle, pain & suffering for psychological damage.

If an owner's dog is attacked by another dog, the owner can sue for cost of treatment such as vet bills & dog training.

Dog training is to deal with the behavioral change in their dog resulting from the attack.

Behavioral change is psychological damage.

What is the basis of the Court in awarding costs for dog training?

Is the Court quantifying training as psychological or material damage?

Ergo psychological injury to the dog exceeds the dog being property.

The simple legal framework for the recognition of functional sentience as a limited legal right-to-life utilizing existing case laws, and the Courts having sided with the government when agreeing to kill ("behavioral euthanasia") of shelter dogs deemed "severe psychological distress".

Nero's rescue initially placed him in a foster home where he interacted with other dogs and showed a more playful and innocent side. It was a stark contrast to the years of isolation and suffering he had endured. But his life of dangerous behavior toward strangers, especially men, made it challenging to find him a forever home. I contacted his rescue organization, and we spoke several times. They explained Nero's behavioral dysfunctions in graphic detail and were very surprised I remained a "yes" to adopting Nero. Nero would wait to attack prospective male adopters. He would walk around in the foster's yard. When a man stood close to the fence, Nero would rush them, biting their jackets and trying to drag them over the fence into his yard to kill them. Over 100,000 people had viewed Nero's posts.

One morning, I woke to an urgent message from his rescue. The foster's adult child was visiting from college, sitting on the couch, when Nero walked up and dragged her onto the floor, attacking her. Nero intended to kill her, inflicting significant wounds requiring over 100 stitches. Great Danes can crush a man's forearm with the first bite. The fosters told me they fully understood that Nero's actions were not deliberate, and their family remained supportive of Nero coming to me. The rescue org's founder said, "I'll understand if you've decided not to adopt Nero." I replied, "Please send Nero. I still want to adopt him." I knew my life was 100 percent at risk, yet I knew exactly how to rehabilitate Nero.

After Lincoln's premature death, I was prepared for Nero to live three to six months. I was cautious, not wanting to form too strong an emotional connection. However, my goal was to give Nero genuine love and unconditional care as he lived out the sunset of his life. It was important to give Nero his first true sense of *family*, not for my cathartic grief. Nero would teach me the first rule of rehabilitation: genuine familial love heals the entire spectrum of dysfunctions–the same lesson Lincoln had taught me.

> *To want to save someone's life means you must be willing to sacrifice yourself, despite the reality of being killed.*

When I first met Nero in the cargo terminal at SeaTac, he was beautiful but deeply scarred. His eyes held a distrust of humans and a sense of abandonment, a reflection of the hardships he had endured. It was clear Nero never experienced the kind of understanding and patience he so desperately needed and deserved.

Nero was intact, which doesn't matter to any dog expert. Claims that "You can't teach an old dog new tricks" make me laugh. Nero was a giant dog far beyond behaviorism's "best and brightest minds." My focus was on helping Nero understand that he was safe. I practiced diligently to maintain Nero's physical and mental health, allowing his mind to evolve and thrive through his emotionally complex psychological traumas.

Providing Nero with a reliable and predictable set of my own human behaviors in familiar circumstances allowed Nero to learn to internally contextualize his interactions and idiomatically relative to his former life of abject neglect. I began to teach Nero to comprehend the complexity of his emotions. My *parenting protocols* were developed from Lincoln and again, empirically proven with Nero.

It was night when I picked up Nero. Taking him out of his flight kennel was uneventful. When I opened the rear passenger door on the driver's side of my truck, Nero jumped in spryly. I closed the doors and half-opened the windows. My dear friend Jason and I loaded Nero's kennel into the truck bed.

Jason went to the truck and opened the passenger door, and Nero immediately growled and moved toward him. Jason shut the door. I finished the tie-down and approached the driver's side. I opened the door, saying Nero's name while backing onto my seat. If Nero attacked, he would get my shoulders or the back of my head instead of my face or throat. I worked on addressing my own behavior, which is typical when two individuals interact in a relationship that each one will introspect and thus seek a catharsis of their own healings in what they experience and observe of the other.

From my eight years of Wing Chun training with Sifu Fred Kwok[6], I knew that preparation and predictive anticipation were crucial. I always mentally prepare for interactions to possibly go from bad to worse. Nero's numerous attempts to kill all viciously were driven by a psychological predication. Dog experts must accept the risk of being killed. Addressing this reality helped me put my profound fear into context.

Over time, Nero thrived. His extremely dangerous behavior began to subside.

One early morning, I got up to use the bathroom. The room was pitch black. When I returned to bed, Nero was lying, with his head at the foot of the bed, his back along the length of my leg. As I lay down, I deliberately poked Nero's bum, knowing it would upset him. Nero immediately growled, barked loudly, then quickly swung his head and grabbed the top of mine, nipping

---

[6] waynefredrickson, "Fred Kwok Wing Chun Kung Fu Wooden Dummy Demo Feb 17, 2013," *YouTube*, posted February 21, 2013, https://www.youtube.com/watch?v=OpcpLUKDU2Q

both temples. Some blood trickled. Nero lay back down, expecting me to scream or hit him.

I eschew all training methods, especially alpha/leader/dominance; physical restrictiveness suppresses the flexibility of his emotional considerations. I chose to leave Nero unmuzzled, used only a basic two-inch-wide collar on walks, and gave him free rein at home. I was Nero's protective parent, which meant vigilance had to come from me–not Nero.

The early days were marked by numerous setbacks. Nero's decade of abandonment often overcame him, leading to dangerous moments with me. But I refused to confront Nero and very rarely made him back down. I wasn't going to demean his comprehension of his circumstances when he became angry or dangerous. I knew Nero was yearning for guidance, trust, and protection. I made adjustments. I didn't behave stereotypically as humans would do.

I didn't know Nero couldn't be touched below his collar line. The first time I put on his collar for a walk, I deliberately touched his back. He immediately turned, quickly moving toward me. I backed away. Nero growled. I took a few seconds and re-approached Nero, putting his leash on. Nero could have easily taken me down, but he controlled himself and waited for me to return to put his leash on. Discernment of Nero's cogency structure reflected his brilliance.

Over the weeks, I began touching Nero's back during our reset-hugs. Nero started to change. He realized that I understood his nonverbal communication. I learned that being talkative is disingenuous and extraneous. Instead, I was educationally verbal and repetitively prudent. Trust replaced trauma and abandonment, and Nero's outbursts were less frequent and quicker to resolve together–our journey together was marked by more progress with few setbacks.

Even his rescue, the largest Great Dane rescue on the continent, was surprised at his progress. Five months later, I sent a video of Nero lying on the couch, eating a raw beef bone placed on a towel, my face right beside him as he ate. Something his rescue didn't believe was ever possible.

Everything Nero did had a sense of purpose and determination. Nero evolved from his narrow emotional envelope into a well-adjusted and emotionally loving part of my life. Nero's fears were gradually replaced by confidence.

Nero's dangerous reflexes gave way to his gentler disposition. Nero was walking downtown to off-leash dog parks in his first week. I couldn't help but reflect on the incredible potential that resides within every dog. Nero's story is a testament to the power of patience, compassion, and consciousness. Nero and I shared a profound connection built on trust and mutual respect.

Nero bestowed upon me an unexpected gift: the purest form of education at the pace of predation. He showed me the depth of clarity to think clearly during very dire or life-risking circumstances. His presence debunked notions of impermanence, teaching me that love transcends all timelines. My time together with Nero was a journey of transformation for me.

Though it took two months to rehabilitate, Nero's journey is an inspiring example of resilience and the capacity to learn to trust again. Nero defied the odds as a Great Dane, living to the impressive age of "thirteen years, seven months, and one week–surrounded by close friends in his favorite field. I will forever be grateful to Nero.

Nero taught me Love.

Nero and I share a wagon walk during Nero's last months.

Sammie Tsai

Two months after Nero arrived, cute little Sammie arrived. She was a Formosan Mountain Dog puppy, dumped onto the streets of Taiwan. It is a dangerous country where the use of steel leg-hold traps is prolific and politically condoned. I inquired about adopting a dog in Hsinchu who only has one leg intact. Thank you ACT for Taiwan Animals for your profound compassion.[7]

For Sammie, her disfigurement resulted when she tried to cross a road. A speeding car hit Sammie so brutally that both her hind legs and most of her tail were severed on impact.

Less than a year old and weighing nineteen pounds, Sammie was very shy and had initial issues with hiding food. But after a few months, Sammie learned that food was plentiful, and that snacks came throughout the day and even during the night! Sammie is my "second born." She walks on her front legs and uses a wheelchair.[8] Dogs don't have strong spinal musculature; eventually, Sammie's spine will become arthritic, causing her premature death. Twice, Sammie had a blockage and required major lower intestinal surgery.

Nero and Sammie spent their first year together, aside from an occasional foster. Nero always watched out for Sammie. If she barked at another dog, Nero would rush to stand beside her. These are some of my fondest memories in my entire life.

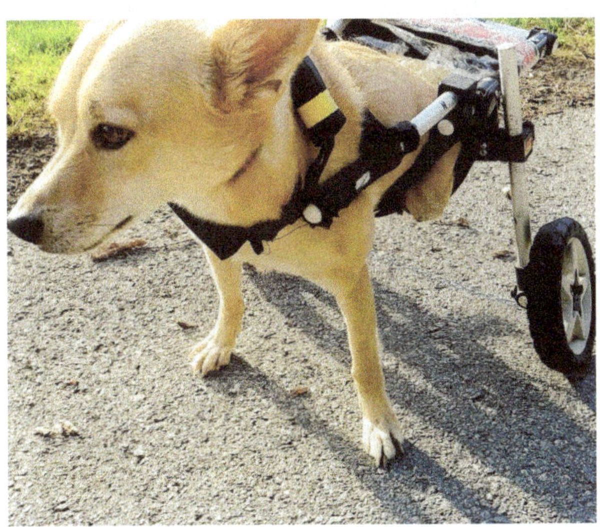

Sammie being the cute girl dog in her wheelchair.

---

[7] ACT for Taiwan Animals, Facebook, posted March 20, 2025, https://www.facebook.com/ACTforTaiwanAnimals/videos/618283734521934/

[8] Arf Arf Bark Bark Rescue & Rehab, "Sammie Was Rescued," *YouTube,* posted April 23, 2018, https://www.youtube.com/watch?v=pRsYDpNZawY

Walter Tsai (Tonka)

Walter is a study of trust and heartbreak. One year later, Walter is a name that will forever hold a special place in my heart. His story is one of resilience, trust, and the unbreakable bond of true family.

Walter emerged as a canvas for charisma. His survival in a world of human anger depended on the unique charm Walter wielded to forge connections. Walter's charismatic nature revealed an understanding of how certain dogs possess an enchanting magnetism. Dogs like Walter taught me about the power of cogency needed for survival; the ability to navigate adversity with a certain charm reveals sophisticated intelligence. Walter's story is one that's deeply intertwined with the complexities of rehabilitation, compassion, and transformation, extending far beyond the reach of behaviorism.

An innocent dog ensnared in the quickening cycle of human abuse, antipathy, and unwantedness. Walter's journey of *self* entailed rebuilding his shattered confidence. I grasped the complex struggle of cultivating trust from the ashes of psychological trauma. Walter was my heartbreaking lesson in trust, set against his history of relentless abuse, forcing me to prove to Walter that he could trust his life to me. Walter was the first in my family-group to say Goodbye.

Though this (standing up) was initiated by Walter in his first week of adoption, his violent reputation had me very trepidatious. Note that I am 5'11" and 190 pounds.

I was trucking to Calgary when I received an urgent message from an acquaintance in California. I called her because she'd forwarded Walter's post. It was about a nineteen-month-old Great Dane at the Southampton Animal Shelter[9], weighing 183 pounds and standing thirty-eight inches at his shoulders.

Walter's history included sixteen attacks. He would end up dragging a shelter worker into his room, attempting to kill her.

Walter lounging on the 5 x 7 rug with Mingki and Nero in the background.

Predation is an evolution tenet. To survive is because of superior contextual intelligence. Giant dogs with diverse predatory histories are extremely rare because they are always the first to be killed. Walter's posts had been seen over 300,000 times. Walter's history of viciousness and "unpredictable" behavior scared an endless list of world-renowned PhD behaviorists, including Ian Dunbar, James Crosby, Rebecca Ledger, Marc Bekoff, Michael Shikashio, Stanley Coren, Michael Ellis, and Karen Pryor. No amount of money offered, nor pleading with them, could inspire help–all admitted Walter was beyond their comprehension. Walter's attacks on sixteen people in New York led to transfers between multiple shelters and homes. Walter faced a short life filled with uncertainty and turmoil as he moved from one

[9] Southampton Animal Shelter Foundation, "Home Page," accessed September 16, 2025, https://southamptonanimalshelter.com/.

home to another, suffering severe abuse in six of seven homes that adopted him.

I contacted his volunteer at the rescue and discussed his case. Walter was back at the shelter, having been returned from his seventh home. Back again, Walter chewed off his own tail midway. It healed, and three weeks later, he chewed the base of his entire tail off, almost bleeding to death overnight. Walter's psychological impairment reflected an extreme dysfunction that universities could only dream of comprehending.

One particular incident highlighted the gravity of Walter's abuses. A shelter worker saw a man dragging Walter out of his car and brutally beating him in the head. Walter was only eight months old. It was during this traumatic episode that Walter suffered brain damage, causing hearing and vision impairments. Another family used a heavy-duty shock collar, bragging about using it at full power when "training" Walter around food. They were laughing that Walter would quiver and drool in fear, backing away from food. Another family adopted Walter and, on the same day, brought him to their son's baseball game but left him in the vehicle. Walter refused to let them in, and he had to be snared by a catch-pole. Another family knew Walter had significant issues with food and promised to be vigilant–yet they allowed their toddler to walk up to him while he was eating. Walter bit the child in the face, and the injury required plastic surgery. Walter required three trainers at Southampton, in case he attacked.

While volunteers were still checking my references, one evening at closing, a staff member was giving nightly treats when Walter grabbed her forearm and dragged her into his room, trying to kill her. She received very serious injuries, yet she did not want Walter killed. I was asked, "Do you want to adopt Walter?"

He had endured hardship and neglect, leaving him with deep-seated dysfunctions, fears, and insecurities. Walter's trust in humans had been repeatedly broken every time another family beat him—one even threatened to use their shotgun. I saw Walter not as a lost cause or just an animal but as an individual desperately in need of help. Seven homes. Each time, he returned to his loneliness at the shelter.

While rescue volunteers were arranging his flight, local animal control suddenly stepped in and sought a court order to kill Walter. They cited two other counties that also had kill orders should Walter return to either county. Walter's case went to trial on Friday, January 13, 2017. Over a hundred people wrote letters to the court asking Walter to be allowed to come to me. The judge allowed Walter to fly to me on one condition: Walter's main volunteer, Pat–an ex-military and ex-NYPD–had to chaperone him. The court also issued a no-return kill order for the state of New York.

They rented a minivan, with Walter and Pat riding in the back on their way to the airport. When they stopped for gas, Pat went inside while their volunteer driver stayed in the minivan. Walter attempted to attack the driver. When Pat came back to the minivan, he saw the driver's back up against the inside of the windshield.

Massive Walter flew to SeaTac in a massive wooden cargo crate donated by Richard Bivens. I met Walter in their hotel lobby. The moment Walter sighted a King German Shepherd across the lobby, he immediately lunged toward him. His handler desperately tried to control him.

I was sitting in a chair when Walter walked over to me, literally looming over my head. He looked down at me, then walked away–only to return, then leave again. Pat told me the driver was in a separate hotel room, refusing to be around Walter. I was deathly scared.

We went to Pat's hotel room to grab Walter's paperwork. Walter was standing by the bed when I entered. Upset, Walter lunged, broke free, quickly rushed me–biting my left forearm and lifting my 190-pound body off the ground, shaking me violently. Anyone who's been attacked by a large predator knows the organically violent, mechanical power of being shaken. It was winter. I wore two pullovers and a thick, heavy winter jacket, but Walter's teeth still cut through, causing lacerations.

We went for a walk. Pat struggled to hold the leash, as Walter repeatedly lunged at me. I walked across the street, but he kept lunging, whether I was in front or behind. I left them alone to see if Walter could calm down. Forty minutes later, he was still lunging–at me and at strangers.

It was getting late so I suggested muzzling Walter and putting him in the back seat of my truck, tethering his leash to the seatbelt so he couldn't get to the front. Pat tethered Walter, as they'd done before, but Walter violently charged, biting two of Pat's fingers through the muzzle. With the truck doors closed, Walter continued lunging, rocking my 9,000-pound dually-truck sideways.

We drove together to see if Walter would settle. Walter continued to lunge at me, and sometimes at Pat. Returning to the hotel, Pat said, "It's okay if you decide to kill Walter today. I've never seen him this bad." Pat said they'll reimburse the vet invoice.

My concerns were for Sammie. Nero, though once extremely vicious, was now eleven years old. He couldn't defend himself against Walter–who was twice his width and eight inches taller. As the sun set during our two-hour drive north, I moved my hand along the center console. Each time, Walter lunged violently. The truck shook on the highway, causing people to stare in amazement. We crossed into Canada and arrived home.

Walter was like a lion and a serial killer. I took numerous precautions at home: placing innocuous items strategically as shields, keeping bedroom doors slightly ajar for a quick escape. Walter would chase me–sometimes stalkingly. I focused on helping Walter overcome his traumatic past. In three days, Walter was off-leash at dog parks. Within five days, Walter approached people for affection. On my social media, people who knew Walter were profoundly surprised. The work within the confines of our home was the most challenging. "Home" was where the inescapable abuses Walter suffered were brutally worse–hidden behind each family's walls.

As each presenting dysfunction was stabilized, deeper layers and facets became more rawly exposed. With Walter's cogency stabilizing, delayering traumas was more painful and emotionally foreign. Walter couldn't contextualize feelings of familial protection and love. All Walter knew of familial protection had been beaten out of him by half a dozen malicious families. Such concentrated abuse–on top of abandonment–would cause a human to adopt severe sociopathy. As Walter began to feel safe and familiar with trusting his emotions, he struggled with visceral confusion, causing him to defend himself. Walter was confused by psychological misinterpretation due to never having had a healthy familial intradependency.

Nearing one year, I changed Tonka's name to Walter. Names for dogs and children foster an emotional and intelligent relationship. *Tonka* wasn't reflective of a highly intelligent and charismatic individual while *Walter* inferred greater comprehension.

Walter's transformation was a testament to the power of compassion and following intuition. Despite the darkness that had defined his first nineteen months, Walter learned to trust again, letting go of predatory, extreme dangerousness. Walter's journey was a remarkable one, a testament to the cogency of dogs and their evolutionary capacity to psychologically heal when given the chance.

Our journey together began slowly, as I spent twenty-four hours a day with Nero, Sammie, and Walter. The wariness in Walter's eyes needed my patience. I knew Walter's trust must be earned, not alpha-demanded.

When I realized Walter was partially blind and deaf, I contacted Pat. I was told about the family brutally beating his head. To help him, I installed LED lights inside and outside the house, to provide a broader light spectrum for Walter's poor eyesight. This meant ensuring twenty-four hours of consistent light, which made sleeping difficult. During the first weeks, I had a "fence" of chairs and an X-pen around my bed.

Mealtimes were brutal. Feeding raw meat diet is evolutionally superior. Walter ate four pounds daily, split into breakfast and dinner, plus snacks. Placing Walter's bowl down, he would instantly turn to attack me. I had to feed Walter in the living room so I could distract him at one side, run to the other side, place his food, then rush back because he'd turn and chase me. Walter is taller, longer, and heavier than a male adult cougar.

Walter doesn't attack to hurt; he attacks cogently. That is predation. Knowing how to behave around Walter, especially when he bit, was crucial. When someone hits another person, they expect the victim to consequentially behave. Walter's function of cogency was still uncouth yet he worked to emotionally and logically make sense of my atypical "human behavior": Walter bit expecting me to respond harshly, as all seven of his previous families had. This is the intelligence of logic and emotional relevance. Instead, I behaved atypically. I remained physically consistent and steady with my VoiceKey. Being bitten by a Great Dane's teeth is extremely painful.

As days became weeks, Walter seemed even more dangerous. He was overwhelmed with new emotions, as circumstances typically caused him terrible trouble. When Walter bit, he expected to get yelled at or beaten. Depending entirely on the circumstances, I'd either continue my same physical route of behavior or pragmatically adjust my behavior and physicality in as natural a manner as possible. If I were bitten by Walter's giant teeth, I'd suppress my pain until I leave the room. Compound bites feel like a hydraulic press.

Our lives became a delicate dance of patience and encouragement. Walter began to comprehend that he was safe and loved by creating a healthy, intradependent familial relationship. I'm vigilant. Outdoors, I kept a vocal connection using Walter's name. I wasn't talking to people with my eyes off of Walter, so he's aware I'm protectively parenting him—studying and learning his personality and psychosomatic manifestations, while comparing them with the behaviors I had seen from Lincoln and Nero.

One sunny afternoon, we were walking in the dog park when a small dog, about seventy-five pounds, came up to Walter. The dog spooked and immediately attempted to bite Walter's face. Walter pulled away. Instead of attacking and killing the dog, he came straight to me, though he kept turning back to see if the other dog would attack him again. I stepped between them immediately, regardless of the danger. The guy didn't apologize. This happened occasionally with irresponsible parents. Walter instead growls warningly at irritating dogs so loudly they shirk away. Walter continued to improve. His interest in prey was stabilized; he no longer chased rabbits or squirrels when off-leash. Predation and prey interest are easy to rehabilitate.

Walter's journey to recovery was far from linear. There were setbacks, moments of fear, and instances where traumas resurfaced. Through it all, I remained steadfast beside Walter. He was sophisticated enough to be aware that his past traumas and present fears emotionally made sense to him. I readjusted my initial rehabilitation time from seven to twelve months to fourteen to nineteen months due to his vision and hearing impairments. If Walter can't recognize a shape, this elicits PTSD. As the months passed, Walter's fears gradually gave way to confidence, and his once-vicious demeanor transformed into warmth and affection. Walter found his forever home within *our* family.

In the first few weeks, it wasn't safe to walk past him. I even needed to carry a folded three-step ladder as a shield just to get through the hallway. I would deliberately wait for Walter's bum to pass me, then reach out and poke him, drawing my hand back as fast as I could while holding the shield. This was super dangerous. Walter turned on the spot and was able to bite my quickly withdrawing hand. He would chase me, and I would run backward into my bedroom at the end of our hallway.

When we moved eighteen months later, I was putting boxes in my little car. After filling up the back, I brought boxes for the front seat. Walter squeezed his massive body into it. It was beautiful and poignant. Walter was cogent;

he knew things in the house were constantly leaving via our car, but I wasn't taking him with me. His self-awareness reflected an introspective sophistication.

Sunday walk on the five-mile Stanley Park Seawall. The park receives over eight million visitors annually.

Walter's life came to an abrupt end on March 1, 2019, when he suffered a massive heart attack during our walk. My beloved Walter was four years and two months old. Walter's death deeply devastated me, especially since I was preparing that Goodbye for Nero (who was thirteen years and four months old at the time). This is my first announcement of Walter's death.

Walter's legacy lives on—a testament to the potential for healing and transformation, even in the face of the most challenging circumstances, and at a time when the whole world around Walter didn't believe.[10]

Looking back on our time together, I am filled with gratitude for the privilege of being part of Walter's life. Walter taught me the resilience for forgiveness

---

[10] For more information about Walter's journey, see the article from the *Vancouver Sun*: https://vancouversun.com/news/local-news/b-c-based-dog-whisperer-to-rehab-great-dane-rescued-by-911-first-responder

and to trust again. Walter's story is a testament to the power of compassion, patience, and the unwavering bond between familial-species.

Walter was the first of my five beloved Great Danes who said Goodbye, breaking my heart each time. My first generation of predatory Great Danes. In the end, it was Walter who gave me the greatest gift–the reminder that with love and understanding, rehabilitation is entirely possible for all dogs with behavioral issues.

Walter taught me Trust.

Lincoln Tsai Jr.

With Lincoln Jr.'s (Sylus) arrival, empathy took center stage. Lincoln's vastly diverse emotional range pushed me to engage with my emotions authentically. His expressive nature became a mirror to my feelings, urging me to embrace empathy as a bridge to comprehension. His parents were breaking up, and Lincoln Jr. had been declared a danger by Vancouver Animal Control. He would drag his dad using his 160-pound body, lunging powerfully with booming, angry barks.

Beautiful Lincoln Jr. stands with his mom with the bravado of a frightened child trying to stay alive in a world that no longer feels safe to him. Watch Lincoln's head flick[11]–the same violence as Nero. The video shows Lincoln pretending to grab Walter's throat sideways, ripping downward. That isn't predation–it's significant cogency in creating personalized, signature behavior. Walter towers seven inches taller, exposing Lincoln Jr. to being attacked from above. Coming into our family would mean that a disagreement could result in a significantly dangerous circumstance.

Lincoln Jr.'s life, which was already crumbling physically, affected him. His expressive emotions and verbal articulation taught me to recognize the high emotional diversity of behavior. Experiences introvertively predicate responses–how the world around them is processed introspectively. I was to learn from Lincoln Jr. how to better understand *our* inner selves. Lincoln

---

[11] Arf Arf Bark Bark Rescue & Rehab, "Great Dane DOG AGGRESSION Deemed DANGEROUS by Animal Control," *YouTube*, posted April 5, 2018, https://youtu.be/opg0YVQPTKA?si=8inhEwU_ufjiX50d

Jr. had bitten me on a few occasions. His huge Great Dane mouth had bitten both sides of my upper thigh... just like Nero's mouth.

I renamed him Lincoln Jr. for his great emotional heart and as a tribute to a remarkable individual who touched broad swaths of mine. Lincoln Jr. taught me facets of behavior and consciousness that once again proved the sameness of psychosomatic manifestations, as seen in Lincoln, Nero, Walter, and Nina.

Lincoln and Nero enjoying a walk.

Lincoln Jr. would constantly swallow toys and clothing. This was my first experience. He would suck on blankets until they were entirely soaked in his saliva. I needed to figure out how to help Lincoln Jr. stabilize his neurosis. Aside from textural context, his low self-esteem and familial abandonment were primary dysfunctions, causing physiological tension in his jaw and head. This is common due to the broad range of immature emotions that individuals experience. Lincoln was attempting to "chew gum" to self-soothe. He wasn't able to find the emotional comfort that he needed from me. Instead, Lincoln Jr. proactively sought something to ease his emotional self-awareness through mastication, being palpable to him. He confirmed that strong cogency is developed through emotional exposure.

I developed Lincoln Jr.'s VoiceKey by saying his name in my normal voice. I gave him sustained reset-hugs frequently to emotionally re-center his dysfunctions. Initially, he would turn and bite me hard on several occasions during walks when he saw other dogs. Touching Lincoln Jr. resulted in being bitten. His lack of physical awareness was consequential to his dysfunctions. His behavior reflected homogeneity–commonality: psychosomatic manifestations of behavior.

A key point with Lincoln Jr. is that I made sure he knew my face wasn't a dangerous weapon, as in verbally abusive. Being yelled at will cause the person's face to be a place of inexplicable emotional anger. This can fixate on which attacking the face occurs. It's typical to be face-to-face, as considered neutral in human domestication, whereas wild or feral dogs practice caution due to personal safety.

Through familial inclusive protection, Lincoln Jr. began to feel safe. I was able to give reset-hugs when he saw dogs. Walter and Lincoln Jr. were able to go together at off-leash dog parks. "Bonded" behavior isn't a real thing.

As I reflect on Lincoln Jr.'s journey, his recent passing weighs heavily on me. Lincoln Jr. passed away in an emergency due to heart failure—a physiological result of prolonged high emotional distress. Lincoln Jr.'s primary doctor failed to recognize his heart murmur over the two years he saw her, including overnight hospitalizations and prolonged periods.

Lincoln Jr. was seven and a half years old when he became part of my family, and he said Goodbye at the age of eleven years, eight months, and two weeks.

Our journey began with consistent, vigilant parental supervision. At the slightest sign of a negative interaction between Walter and Lincoln Jr., I addressed them immediately. I would stop whatever I was doing, immediately physically intervening.[12] There were a few times when Lincoln Jr. irritated Walter; Walter would grab and lift him off his feet. Walter has bowled Lincoln Jr. head-over-paws.[13]

Lincoln Jr. taught me Empathy.

Mingki Tsai

Mingki's presence served as a reminder of temporality. Mingki had been born to be a meatdog on one of the hundreds of filthy South Korean meatdog farms. Meatdogs are "ripe" at around two years old and are

---

[12] You may read more about this here: http://bit.ly/4ny8lsW.

[13] Arf Arf Bark Bark Rescue & Rehab, "DANGEROUS DOG - German Shepard Bites People, Attacks Other Dogs," *YouTube*, posted July 19, 2018, https://www.youtube.com/watch?v=laGKEyiNHJ0&t=590s

horrifically tortured prior to death "to enhance their meat." This is uncouth peasantry and conflicts commensurately with Korea's technological advancements.

Mingki couldn't be touched or walked. Stress defecation. Mingki attacked all the dogs and even the staff and visitors at the Animal Hope and Wellness Foundation (AHWF) in Los Angeles. AHWF had been working with some behaviorism universities, but none would accept Mingki. Ian Dunbar declared Mingki "no hope," and although Cesar Millan had done a segment on AHWF, he declined to work with Mingki.

Mingki bears heavy scars of torture on his body, head, and near his eyes. This torture really is normal for South Korean meatdogs. His profoundly abject dysfunction stemmed from a highly narrow emotive envelope, cemented by residential trauma.

When Mingki arrived at SeaTac cargo, his beautiful white Jindo fur was covered in feces and urine. Mingki was very angry and profoundly scared. I stood in the parking lot, worried that Mingki might bolt, get hit by a car, or get lost forever. I couldn't get close to the kennel without Mingki attacking the door. This video playlist showcases Mingki's first thirty-six hours to one week with me.[14]

Mingki in a cage in the South Korean meatdog farm before he was rescued.

[14] Arf Arf Bark Bark Rescue & Rehab, "Dangerous Rescue Dog Mingki #1 - Animal Hope and Wellness Foundation," *YouTube*, posted June 5, 2018, https://www.youtube.com/watch?v=BeRoYnDbKg0&list=PLK43vpl6h3zaCF_Vea06E9btsQB53VSWQ&index=2

His very limited emotional cogency requires significant patience to untangle profound, complex societal and self-aware limitations. Mingki's "meatdog farm" emotional range taught me how to patiently navigate his unfamiliarity with expressing emotions. Essentially, his emotive structure was encased within a cement pipe. Mingki arrived three months after Lincoln Jr.

Sammie and Mingki (l) on my bed.

Fireworks, with their thunderous explosions, terrify many dogs. For Mingki, they were debilitating. I addressed his terror by providing safety and familial inclusion, addressing the important psychological predicate of such a profound fear of fireworks.[15] Mingki is calm, nor is anyone else barking, hence consciousness homogeneity.

William Tsai (Shaggy)

William, a Great Dane from Mexico, has his body marked by abandonment and starvation. His hips were quite displaced due to unlicensed backyard breeding, causing his rear legs to splay in a duck-walk motion. After his family moved, they tied William to a tree in their backyard—no water, no food. He was severely starved, but no one knew he was left behind until his barking drew attention. A Mexican dog rescue restored him to health, and from there, he came to Canada, where the Canadian rescue had given him the demeaning name "Shaggy."

His new adopters ignored instructions to let William adjust and immediately introduced him to other dogs. One dog, scared of William's size, attacked

---

[15] Arf Arf Bark Bark Rescue Foundation, "Fireworks (part 2 of 2)," Facebook, posted July 2, 2018, https://www.facebook.com/share/v/1GaUse1ctt/

him. Hours later, the family again introduced William to another strange dog, which also attacked. These incidents caused William to become very scared; he began barking and lunging at every dog.

His rescue called me. Lisa Gaye, founder of Furever Freed Dog Rescue Society, threatened to kill William if I didn't agree to take him in. She refused to pay for his rehab and repeated that I take William—or she would kill him that evening. She actually mulled sending William back to Mexico, but said it would be cheaper to kill him here—monsters posing as rescuers.

William was 120 pounds thin. I helped him gain a healthy weight of 160 pounds, standing thirty-four inches at the withers. When William saw dogs, small animals, or people, he would walk calmly, then suddenly turn, trying to attack. William would bite and violently shake even King German Shepherds.

William's time in my life was unexpected, yet it made our home full: Nero, Sammie, Walter, Lincoln Jr., Mingki, and William. Every Great Dane—ranging from extremely dangerous to entirely predatory—lived together, free-range, and eating raw together, and sleeping together in the same bedroom—our family-group.

William was very "bitey" when it came to snacks—his bite, powerful like Walter's but faster, sometimes even drawing blood. Since William's long jaw blocked his eyesight, he had to "imagine" where my hand was when targeting a handheld snack. Another reason for snapping is when people throw food at their dogs, which skews perspective and coordination for velocity targeting. William was learning to judge both the distance and textural context of various foods. Snapping, by default, catches the item despite not knowing its physical composition until it's assessed by the tongue and mouth. Snapping is common with dysfunctional dogs.

William was very worried. William was extremely skittish on walks, constantly darting sideways—it was clear he had never gone walking before. Despite this, William was so jovial. However, when William saw other dogs from a distance, he would frantically bark, trying to escape his collar to attack them. William's lack of beneficial social interactions resulted in awkwardness that confounded his emotional processing. His scale of consciousness and cogency processed emotional value in an idiomatically contextual manner, learning from his experiences.

Lincoln watches William with his favorite toy.[16]

William learned he would never go hungry and would always live inside my home. I rehabilitated William's hips simply by enforcing very slow walks for many months. This was very challenging due to William's very wild physicality. The speed of slow walking forced him to begin more natural gait patterns. This slower pace also reduced his emotional concern about feeling safe in public. The best physiotherapy is walking dogs very slowly for ten minutes or even for the whole walk. Over our first two years together, William developed a fuller stride range and darted far less. Enforcing slow walks also meant that William urinated less frequently and eventually stopped altogether.

Lincoln Jr. and William were hypersensitive to touch. Both flinched when touched, even while sleeping, yet neither attacked when disturbed during sleep. Flinching as a dysfunction is due to human abuse, often by a "leader." Being touched correlates context of self-awareness. This analogous dysfunction of oppressive abuse, contrary to family-group structure, supported William's fear of being beaten. His level of impatience is human analogous. This affectation on humans is similarly scaled. Psychological and physical oppression, such as "flipping your dog onto their back," profoundly retards emotional broadness and maturation.

Then came Anthony, a two-year-old, 170-pound blue Great Dane, originally named Brutus. He came from a Great Dane rescue in California. Erika Calle, the founder of One Dane At A Time, Inc., begged and begged me to rehab Anthony for free (once Anthony was here, Erika stopped taking my calls and messages). Anthony was highly destructive if left alone and would kill any

---

[16] Ark Arf Bark Bark Rescue Foundation, "My dearest William Tsai," *Facebook*, posted September 2, 2023, https://www.facebook.com/share/v/1MYUd6uf52/

dog. He was very energetic and young. After the initial period of fights and disagreements, Anthony realized that fighting was not necessary because I sustained vigilant parental supervision.

Anthony was quite a prankster. Anthony loved to be in the backyard, waiting for William to pee or poop. When William went bathroom, Anthony would sprint full speed and knock him over! Anthony thought it hilarious and would dance around, hoping William would chase him. William, however, was very offended and eventually stopped going to the bathroom whenever Anthony was outside. William stopped playing with Anthony. I addressed this by standing protectively by William at all times he was in the backyard, and block Anthony. William would get angry at Anthony, barking and trying to bite him when Anthony came too close.

A few months later, Anthony was transfer-exchanged when David arrived. William happily ran around teasing Walter, Lincoln Jr., and even Nero.

When Walter died, William experienced significant grief. I helped William process grief along with my own. I maintained the same tones and behaviors as much as I could. With Walter being our family-group's first death, preventing grief from becoming a residential emotive structure in everyone was imperative. Lincoln Jr. and William became lonely. Their exhibition of grief (the objective awareness that *someone is missing*) proved homogeneous. William exhibited grief after the deaths of Walter, Nero, and Lincoln Jr.

The year following Lincoln Jr.'s death, William was diagnosed with cancer. Fifteen days later, William died. As the cancer spread, William would hide to defecate. Fresh blood was found in his stools during the last two days of his life. William would hide in the bushes to defecate because his internal pain was so bad that he was unable to process the severe, intense pain of cancer despite being on heavy pain medication. Familial-species feel emotionally alone when they are dying.

William's death was excruciatingly slow under the hands of the same veterinarian who had overseen Lincoln Jr. and failed to diagnose his obvious heart murmur. Dr. Renu admitted she didn't own a needle long enough to reach William's heart, which had shifted further from the chest wall due to fluid congestion in his lungs. Despite knowing this, she futilely pushed through. Yet she still failed to reach William's heart and injected aimlessly. For forty-one minutes, William suffered as she repeatedly injected William's legs, tongue, and chest–each time failing. It was horrifying to witness profound ineptitude. William remained alive through repeated attempts, enduring a drawn-out, torturous death.

The most deficiently unprofessional thing I have ever heard a veterinarian say came from her mouth: she told me she was running out of solution and would need to drive back to her clinic–twenty minutes away–to refill. That would have meant at least another hour of William lying in a comatose state in front of me.

At that time, I was friends with a well-known animal activist. Jen, who hosts an animal welfare podcast and has interviewed Paul Watson, asked to be present at William's scheduled death, claiming she wanted to offer me emotional support. Instead, she turned out to be a morbid individual. She took pictures of William's final hours and then refused to forward his photos to me for four months. William's life is tainted with my guilt for allowing these two individuals to wreck my precious last moments with William.

William leaves his life's testament to the resilience all dogs possess when a caring human is willing to help a severely dysfunctional dog heal. William had just turned eight years old. I always thought William would live to at least twelve–and certainly not die miserably. Even now, William's presence continues to unfold in my work.

William taught me Time.

David Tsai (Gryffin)

The closure of my beloved first-generation, David[17] is the last of my family's generation. Walter was 183 pounds, whereas David was 211 pounds. Both Harlequins, both stood thirty-eight inches at the shoulders. David bit sixteen times, whereas Walter attacked sixteen times. David had his entire tail.

When William first saw David, William came from the bedroom through the hallway, and David from the other end. William's eyes widened with the shock of recognizing someone familiar face-to-face. William looked at David, recognizing him, then came the realization, it wasn't Walter. It had been eight months since Walter's death. Sammie seeing David, on the other

[17] James Tsai, "How Huge Is Gryffin?" Facebook, https://www.facebook.com/share/r/1VVfDPRzDe/

hand, was different. Small as she was, Sammie noticed David's smaller paws. Sammie's recognition was, "Oh great...another dog," then she walked away.

David had grown up with a single parent and a young child. The child would run down in the mornings and jump on David while he was sleeping. Later, David was boarded with a well-known police-dog trainer in the South, who had fancy trucks and a glamorous presence on social media. His ineptitude caused significant dysfunctional harm to David. The police trainer shattered David's stability with the concepts of "alpha" and "forced submission." He transformed David's familial life into one of discipline through alpha-dominance. This is analogous to being cohabitatively controlled.

David was two and a half years old. His rescue drove 2,600 miles from Indiana in three days. David had been prescribed 80 mg of Prozac and 750 mg of Trazodone for two years. Serotonin syndrome occurs with most psychopharmaceuticals, forcing behavioral default of fogged cogency. Ironically, "side effects include aggression." Bobbi Jo Becker, founder of Tails of Freedom K9 Rescue, made the drive.[18] I'm grateful she saved David when no one wanted him. Bobbi Jo's emails to other giant-dog rescue organizations, master dog trainers, and behaviorists–such as Michael Shikashio, Marc Bekoff, and Ian Dunbar–all came back with the same advice: that David should be killed, as he had exceeded their standards.

In a year, David was able to bring himself to sit beside me on the couch or the bed. Letting me run my hand along his body. Initially, David would turn toward me, bite, then leave. Patience is crucial. Everyone sets expectations and strives for progress, but any pushback from their dog causes people to become offended or indignant. The human demand for instant gratification is a bane. If a bite happens, frustrations and intense emotions rage from the human. The human feels upset, and its distrust of their dog increases, because of a bite, which alters the emotional relationship in noticeable ways. Yet, it is not a remarkable event (the bite) to their dog. Afraid of being bitten again, it (the human) may either immediately disengage from its dog–leaving the room or behaving disingenuously in showing physical affection. Their dog comprehends body language and emotional communication. David, sitting beside me on the couch, made a remarkably cogent decision: David overcame his emotional immaturity and was accepting familial intimacy.

---

[18] Here is David's rescue: https://www.facebook.com/share/p/1BPLK5jpGp/

When David bit me, I would remain in place to remonstrate his expectation of punishment: yelling, screaming, beating, or being exiled outside or locked in a kennel for hours. By contrast, canine inter-social punishment doesn't last for hours. The psychological endurement of complex emotives doesn't plausibly exist in the wild.

First week of David's arrival (still very skinny at 180-ish pounds instead of 211 pounds).

David meeting super hyper Tarcin the Golden Retriever.

I've learned that physical and psychological experiences can inspire intuition or cloud it. Fear stems from the inability to feel safe, and self-protection becomes extreme. David's size was ominous to everyone. I knew significant cogency within dogs means mouths and tongues are highly contextual and textural. Any nip or bite is brief and precise in pattern, reflecting significant control relative to the speed pattern of the bites. An attack, however, is much different than a bite or nip, regardless of size. David's sixteen bites indicate his potential for predation as highly *unlikely*, relative to the consistency of circumstances. Even if he returned to the same consistent environment and issues, without further exacerbation, David still wouldn't.

I was in the kitchen. It's small, with a triangle-shaped island that can fit only one Great Dane. David's been here four months. While I was cleaning up after dinner, David came to see me. Lincoln Jr. and William approached from either side, thinking there was more food, and unintentionally crowded David. Standing close beside me, I reached toward David. He immediately took my hand in his mouth and applied strong, steady pressure on the bones. I relaxed on purpose as his mouth's pressure was consistent, which indicated cogency. I worried David might inadvertently fracture my hand. I didn't strike or yell. I told Lincoln Jr. and William to leave the kitchen, which they did. David let go on his own.

Compound pressure from David's teeth cut two rectangle tooth marks, and it took a month before I could use my hand functionally, another two months to use it with ease. David felt claustrophobic and unfamiliar. I maintained a consistent VoiceKey, then followed up with a reset-hug for David.

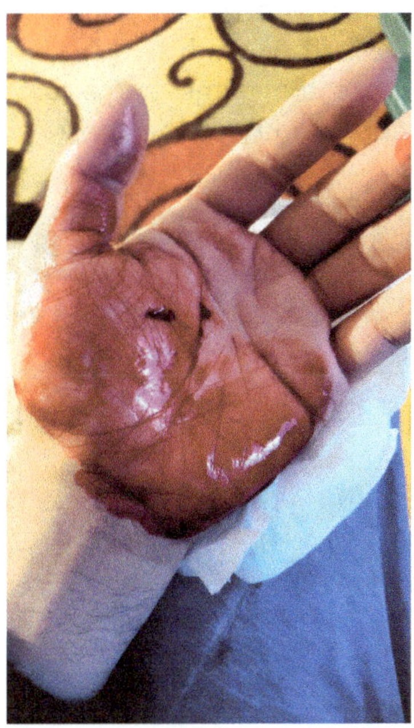

After David's compound pressure bite (re: Lincoln Jr. and William)

Over time, David began to feel safer, often seeking me for reset-hugs whenever he felt unsafe. I also contextualized reset-hugs when David faced complex foreign emotive confusions. David no longer bucked up and down anymore; instead, he came to me for reset-hugs. Reset-hugs on walks take longer due to the unfamiliar emotive environment. David's difficult family life–oppressive board-and-train experience, and two years of heavy medication–took a severe toll on him. He also arrived with a heart murmur. In early 2024, on an early spring morning, David collapsed from a heart attack in front of me. David was almost six years old.

David taught me Sadness.

Aby (Pacific Rim Rescue, WA)

Aby the Weimaraner boarded as a long-time foster and was around five to six years old. Aby shared two years here before she was adopted late 2024. Originally founded by Mindi Person and Alec Strigen, Pacific Rim Rescue in Washington[19] saved Aby's life in many, many ways.

Aby and her sister, Nora, lived in an unlicensed breeder's backyard in Mexico, confined to a small, filthy dirt enclosure with broken cement. Both were severely emaciated, their ribs and spines clearly visible, and had endured multiple pregnancies. Aby's front teeth had been extracted, and her side teeth were ground down to the gums. Procedures are typically done by unlicensed backyard breeders without anesthesia or pain relief.

Aby and her sister Nora in Mexico prior to rescue.

[19] Pacific Rim Rescue LLC, "Home Page," accessed September 16, 2025, https://pacificrimrescue.org/

Aby was really good friends with William and David. For two years, we walked together in the Nature Park. I heavily considered adopting Aby each time after their deaths. But I knew it would have been a selfish decision. Aby had already lived a horrific life, yet she loved to be loved. Aby deserved an exclusive family of her own, not a life where she constantly had to share and compete for my attention.

Aby was not used to walking–her front and back legs moved together in an uncomfortable waddle. She developed two growths beside her nipples and an enlarged spleen, originally feared to be cancerous, just like William's. Mindi discussed with her board about fundraising $6,000 for Aby's splenectomy. Mindi was adamant that Aby would have her own family. I am honored to have worked with Pacific Rim Rescue.

Aby thrives with her new family and will forever remain in my Soul. While reviewing the final manuscript edits of my book, I was informed by Mindi that Aby's cancer returned and metastasized with terminal prognosis.

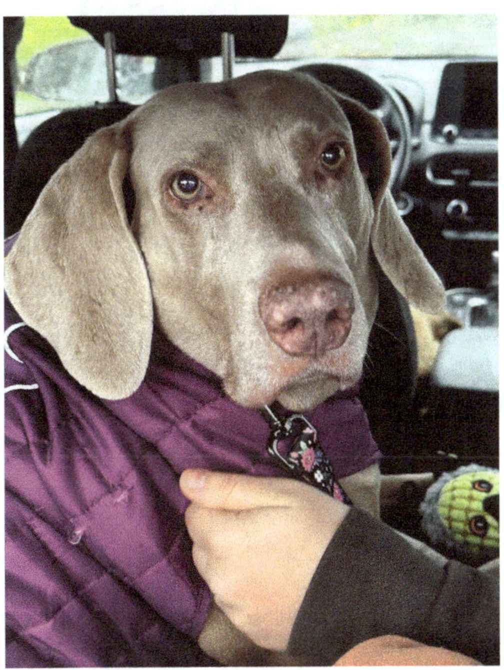

Aby with her new family in Washington

Life with Dysfunctional Predatory Dogs

Feeding my canine family is a substantial undertaking, involving approximately 750 pounds of raw meat each month. My own dietary choices, however, were influenced by Lincoln, my first beloved Great Dane. Out of respect for their lives and the compassion they've taught me, I've chosen not to eat meat. I couldn't fully immerse myself in rehabilitating predation while also being a carnivore, as it removes all nuance of empathy beneficial to anthropomorphic intuition. It's important for my cogency relative to my evolutional construct.

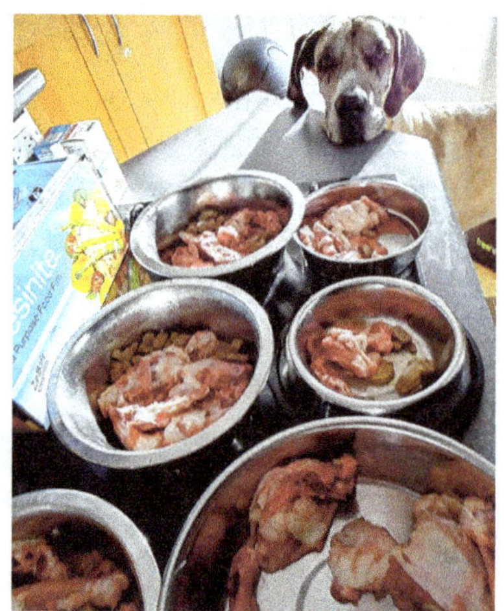

William waiting for dinner

My approach is rooted in principles of familial inclusion and healthy dependencies. I say everyone's name in chronological seniority, emphasizing them as members of a family-group. This fosters a sense of familial belonging within the group and our household as a family unit for idiomatic contextualization.

I don't make anyone wait for meals. It needlessly creates insecurity about food. It's obtuse to think that dogs don't comprehend that I'm providing nourishment parentally.

When one of my beloveds approaches their Sunset, I return to the familiar tones and practices from our earliest days together. This sustains a sense of self and revisits the significance of our family. Through their lives and struggles, I've garnered insights into loss, love, trust, empathy, transience, cogency, abandonment, and charisma. The journey continues, the pages unfold, and with every dysfunctional dog that enters my life, a new chapter of wisdom is taught to me.

At the heart of my work lies a resolute belief that the academia's grasp of dog behavior is fundamentally flawed. These misconceptions have led to misguided practices and, tragically, the needless killings euphemistically termed "euthanasia" of dogs deemed "beyond hope." I believe my unique approach to comprehending consciousness and behavior can reshape this field.

You can learn about my most recent adoption and see what I specifically look for when adopting on my Facebook page.[20]

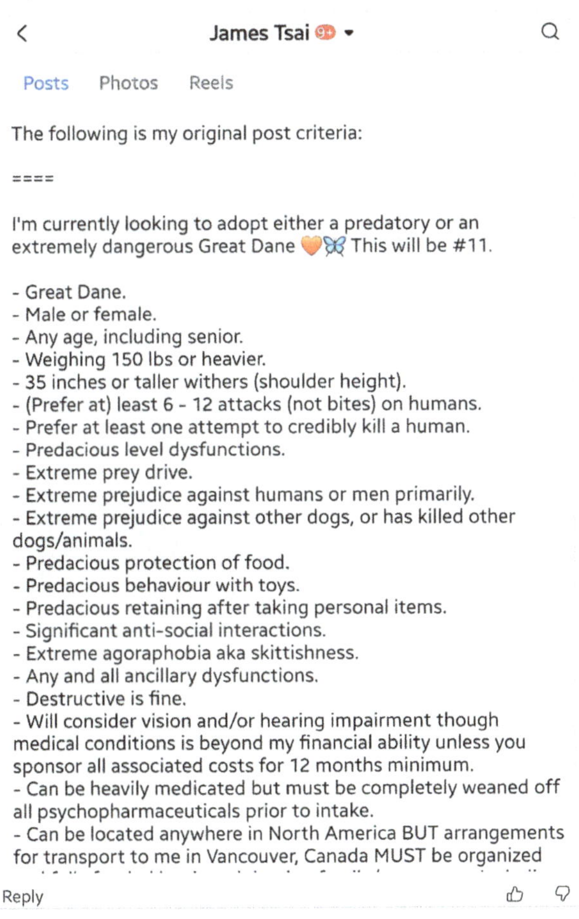
James Tsai 9+

Posts Photos Reels

The following is my original post criteria:

====

I'm currently looking to adopt either a predatory or an extremely dangerous Great Dane 🧡🦋 This will be #11.

- Great Dane.
- Male or female.
- Any age, including senior.
- Weighing 150 lbs or heavier.
- 35 inches or taller withers (shoulder height).
- (Prefer at) least 6 - 12 attacks (not bites) on humans.
- Prefer at least one attempt to credibly kill a human.
- Predacious level dysfunctions.
- Extreme prey drive.
- Extreme prejudice against humans or men primarily.
- Extreme prejudice against other dogs, or has killed other dogs/animals.
- Predacious protection of food.
- Predacious behaviour with toys.
- Predacious retaining after taking personal items.
- Significant anti-social interactions.
- Extreme agoraphobia aka skittishness.
- Any and all ancillary dysfunctions.
- Destructive is fine.
- Will consider vision and/or hearing impairment though medical conditions is beyond my financial ability unless you sponsor all associated costs for 12 months minimum.
- Can be heavily medicated but must be completely weaned off all psychopharmaceuticals prior to intake.
- Can be located anywhere in North America BUT arrangements for transport to me in Vancouver, Canada MUST be organized

Reply

[20] http://bit.ly/4n8Wd1M

CHAPTER 3

Unveiling My Calling

I was drawn into the realm of rescue organizations, where my unfiltered honesty often collided with politics. This journey was characterized by a deep-seated understanding that dogs are functional sentient beings. My unique perspective, devoid of conventional training methods, empirically establishes profound quantifiable communication between familial-species, including dogs and humans.

Recognizing my distinct gift was not a straightforward path. I regarded my progress with Lincoln as an achievement accessible to all. Despite receiving praise, I struggled to accept that I possessed a gift that set me apart.

Educating people about my work became a necessity, driven by the unyielding desire to save dogs from needless "euthanasia." I found myself surrounded by ignorance and miscomprehension. Dog experts, trainers, behaviorists, and dog owners are often ignorant of the potential to rectify all dysfunctions. I recognize the urgency to dispel the misconceptions. My purpose crystallized: to challenge conventional thinking, modernize behaviorism, and elevate dogs' standing in society rather than deem them "disposable property."

Reshaping the field means deconstructing the pedestals of false icons and challenging establishments that accredit who continue to perpetuate misguided, failed methodologies. By imparting knowledge about the corresponding diluted scale and construct of consciousness, I aim to bring humanity closer to comprehending itself and achieving genuine Artificial Intelligence *consciousness*.

My calling entails spearheading a movement to advocate for the legal recognition of dogs and cats as functionally sentient. This struggle encompasses our species, our planet, and our collective future. While my work lays the foundation, I trust forthcoming generations will advance my theorem.

Part 2
What We Know

CHAPTER 4

Domesticated Companions: The Timeless Bond Between Dogs and Humans

We'll embark on a journey through the ages, reviewing the parallel steps of our two species. From the very dawn of our existence, dogs have transcended mere companionship. They have been our hunting partners, our allies, our confidants, and even our surrogate children. We've shown that, ultimately, we *are* caring and familially protective. This wasn't just a matter of convenience; it was a profound connection shaped by mutual benefit and shared experiences. This shows that dogs' brains have an evolutionally developed framework of emotive-isomorphism, causal for broadly psychological familial relationships. This is akin to (adaptive) introgression.[21]

As humans shifted to an agrarian way of life, the selective breeding of dogs for human companionship is misconceived as the foundation for cross-species domestication. The construction for comprehending and conforming to cohabitative domestication is homogeneous, scaled isomorphic by the manner of emotional comprehension. This proves each dog's individual consciousness capacity to independently understand and sustain highly complex, though often disingenuous, cross-species relationships—an ability wrongly treated as fatally disposable, even as we utilize their natural talents to serve our evolving needs.

Key to comprehending the phylogenesis of consciousness is the recognition that "consciousness" itself is functionally intradependent and conflates behavioral flow (and any terms we assign to it, such as cognition, cogency, or logic). Dogs guarded livestock without predation and, at times, even developed friendships with such "prey." They patrolled our settlements, lending their keen senses to warn us of impending danger. Through this

[21] https://en.wikipedia.org/wiki/Introgression

shared journey, our emotional symbiotic relationship was born—paving the way for the co-evolution of familial-species.

History doesn't literate whether wild dogs opposed human cohabitation at any time, even during Pavlov's deliberately fatal dog experiments. Moral and ethical conflicts are sacrificed for what ultimately turns out to be academic miscomprehension. As to domiciling domestication, were dogs not conforming to living with humans then shunned, cast outside the tent, or killed? Thirty-thousand years ago, dogs were primal predators. Yet early humans created crude familial-social structures across species, proving that predation is not intransigent among familial-species and knowingly accommodating contrived. They imposed disingenuous relationships with another apex species. The 20th century cohabitative domestication marked a contrived turning point in our history. The early humans chose dogs for dependency, companionship, and partnership instead of material utility.

It's inept to opine that "humans domesticated dogs"[22] 30,000 years ago—or even today. Most cohabitating dogs are neutered. It's impossible to influence "co-living with humans." Neutered dogs can't have offspring. There is no evolutional assistance by humans. Emotional isomorphism is inherent in all familial-species, at a corresponding dilutive scale. It's impossible for early humans to "tame" a few early wild dogs (wolves), resulting in evolutionary extrapolation. Early humans would have needed to exert control over the entire physical region containing much larger populations of all wild dogs. Nor could a few individual dogs, after direct interaction with humans, simply go back to their family-group and somehow influence "domesticated" traits.

Dogs didn't learn "domestication", no matter the evolutional time scale. This hubristic semantic fails to logically comprehend that there was no manner of sophisticated mechanical transport 30,000 years ago other than the utilization of "the wheel" for travel. Nor would there be an infective virulent influence upon a handful of early, human-friendly wolves who could have dispersed across vast regions of hundreds of miles to progenically influence "domesticated traits" through heredity. Early-wolves were not influencing other wolf family-groups in this way. Nor could one wolf family-group have "taught" or demonstrated domesticated behavior to others on a micro scale sufficient to alter the specie as a whole.

---

[22] http://bit.ly/41VSo7x

How could the ten wolves articulate a "human" context?

The very reason for cross-species cohabitation lies not in the misnomer "learned behavior," but in emotive isomorphism—a shared, homogenous structure for processing emotion.

As human societies evolutionally shifted, the roles of dogs were reshaped—often forcibly. Dogs are burst predators, not endurance predators. Sled dogs were oppressively forced to traverse icy expanses most of their lives and then killed if injured or middle-aged. Herding dogs were left to guide livestock alone, utilized as property for human convenience. These histories reveal both the irony and the tragedy: dogs proved endlessly adaptable as a workforce, yet at the same time held a deep, visceral loyalty to the very specie that exploited them.

Through eras of growth, turmoil, and progress, dogs have stood by our side, providing unwavering support and friendship despite the mercurial punishments the human-specie forced them to face. The human-specie's darkest shadow lies within the braggadocious concept of "domestication" and the legal bukh of judges that dogs are property. Exploitation, neglect, and cruelty continue unabated until they lead to major human self-extinction, marring our legacy of companionship in the interim. This long, dark chapter poignantly reminds us of the failure of responsibility—toward the creatures whose literal lives we have arbitrarily placed in our hands.

Instead, we must honor the timeless bond we share—a bond that transcends the boundaries of familial-species, speaking to the intrinsic connection that higher intelligence humans have in recognizing the sentience of familial-species. In each dog, we find echoes of a story that's as old as humanity itself—the stories of friendship, resilience, and the enduring beauty of a partnership that continues to stand the test of time, though always experienced on an individual level.

CHAPTER 5

Outcast Dogs and Animal Shelters: Rescuing Lives, Restoring Hope

The intricate tapestry of our shared histories unfolds a deeply moving story—one that is hidden from the spotlight but deserves our attention. It's a tale of dogs who, for various reasons, find themselves cast aside, left to navigate the human world that they cannot yet understand, and their psychological struggles. Let's delve into the world of outcast dogs and the sanctuaries of hope that are no-kill animal shelters.

As our anecdotal connection evolved over mere centuries, so too have the challenges politicians are willing to force dogs to face. Our increasingly urbanized landscapes, shifting societal dynamics, and unforeseen circumstances have led to tens of thousands of dogs being abandoned and left to fend for themselves. In many second and third-world countries—such as China, India, across Africa, the Middle East, and Romania—political arrogance and open acceptance of profound cruelty to animals remain rampant. Conflicting with their utility of dogs sustains human-specie disingenuousness. Left adrift, dogs often find themselves on an inescapable solitary journey through crowded city streets and barren rural landscapes, struggling daily for survival. Scarcity of food, exposure to elements, and encounters with danger mark their days, testing their intelligence and often foretell the ending of their lives. Turkey has killed two million stray dogs in less than two years while defrauding the public, claiming Istanbul is kind to stray dogs.

The average homeless dog has a lifespan of two years. Their short lives end through starvation, vehicle collision, deliberate shootings by lesser-evolved humans (lower-boolean human taxa), poisoning, and attacks from other strays and predators. Yet the greatest killer of these outcast dogs is animal control. Politicians, ever prevaricating, ignore the simple empathy required to address overpopulation. What is needed is a federal licensing of all breeders—whether for profit or by "accident." Such regulation would teach the public that having a dog is a privilege, not a right, and that breeding carries legal responsibility.

I've had the worst experience with Canadian politician and former Member of Parliament Ken Hardie. Before an election, he invited me to his office to discuss my petition[23] to make it illegal to eat dog and cat meat in Canada, professing to care. Ken's manipulation exemplifies how willing Canadians are to lie. He used the misery of dogs to get re-elected.

Animal shelters generally are no-kill or kill. In major US cities such as those in Texas, California, and New York, many so-called shelters kill more than 100,000 unwanted dogs annually–*per shelter*.

By contrast, no-kill shelters are ethical havens–places of second chances, where discarded Souls are given life. They are sustained by a dedicated community of individuals who pour their hearts out, providing solace, care, and a glimmer of light to those whom the government has left behind. No-kill shelters host a symphony of stories longing to be heard.

> *Pulling back the curtains of no-kill and kill shelters, we uncover one simple reality: their existence stems from overpopulation, driven by politically supported, unlicensed breeding.*

Stretching resources thin imposes tremendous strain on staff and volunteers, who work tirelessly even though a small number of dogs are ever fortunate to be adopted. Inside those walls, life-and-death decisions are made daily. Meanwhile, tens of thousands of unlicensed breeders are given tacit political encouragement. Shelters whose upper management gives "thumbs up or thumbs down" carte blanche decisions, knowing the public's inability to pursue inexpensive arbitration.

My advocacy to save Echo, a Great Dane, was maliciously thwarted by the cruelty of Colorado's Ark-Valley Humane Society's affluent board of directors and their shelter's manager, Amber van Leuken. Despite my offer to take Echo in my care–and despite several Great Dane rescue organizations stepping forward–van Leuken refused to grant Echo a new lease on life. My

---

[23] Here's a link to my petition: https://www.change.org/p/make-it-illegal-to-eat-dogs-and-cats-in-canada

repeated phone calls and emails to Governor Jared Polis and his husband, Marlon, were ignored.

I pointed out Amber van Leuken's personal Facebook post, where she bragged about flying her young children to Nepal to witness live animal sacrifices. Nepal cruelly hosts an archaic peasantry of their infamously cruel Gadhimai Festival, in which the country literally kills between 500,000 to 1,000,000 animals over just one weekend. Under van Leuken's management, the number of shelter dogs and cats killed at Ark-Valley Humane Society increased by 600 percent. Important news coverage of this issue includes articles from KKTV[24] and Ark Valley Voice.[25, 26]

An unspoken toll–one begging for a class action lawsuit–is the severe psychological distress on shelter staff and volunteers. The system creates irreparable emotional and psychological despair, a reality lived by the staff and volunteers, which is entirely preventable through a simple conversion to no-kill policies and federal licensing of breeders. Many staff are forced to sign non-disclosure agreements under the threat of losing their jobs, while volunteers are forced to remain silent out of fear of being banned. I believe there exists great legal peril if class action lawsuits were filed by shelter staff and volunteers for suffering preventable psychological trauma from dog killings.

My book's empirical work contains very simple guides to addressing dysfunctions. Behavior is homogeneously predicated at a corresponding dilutive scale across all familial-species relative to biological sophistication; hence, consciousness abstraction is scaled. Sophisticated consciousness is repeatedly killed at animal shelters.

A dog born into neglect and abuse reflects not only their suffering but also our morality, our social acceptance, and our tolerance for materialist-

---

24 KKTV, "Previous Owners Fight to Save Colorado Dog's Life While Humane Society Explains Why It Should Be Euthanized," February 13, 2023, https://www.kktv.com/2023/02/13/previous-owners-fight-save-colorado-dogs-life-while-humane-society-explains-why-it-should-be-euthanized/

25 Ark Valley Voice, "Offer to Save Echo Includes New Home and Training in Canada," February 17, 2023, https://arkvalleyvoice.com/offer-to-save-echo-includes-new-home-and-training-in-canada/

26 Ark Valley Voice, "We're His People, and We Want Echo Back," February 10, 2023, https://arkvalleyvoice.com/were-his-people-and-we-want-echo-back/

predation behaviorism. In Texas, Governor Greg Abbott refused to sign strengthened animal cruelty laws until obsequiously seeking reelection. His callousness toward both dogs and children seems rooted in a bitter personal narrative—his preventable accident during a windstorm left him in a wheelchair, and his response appears to be: "Your suffering is no less than my suffering." But cruelty, even when rationalized, is never absolved in God's eyes. Colorado's duplicit politicians are creating laws to kill dogs they have ineptly deemed as "severely psychologically distressed." Amidst challenges and triumphs, one thing is clear: the profound impact of second chances is also a fundamental aspect of being human. The world of dog rescue is a testament to the unyielding spirit of the few.

Our intricate dog-human relationships are reminders of our responsibility as apex dominion predators. It is a call to compassion, education, and advocacy—an invitation to stand united in reshaping the lives of these remarkable beings. We have full power to restore hope, heal wounds, and create a world where no dog is left to navigate their emotional darkness alone.

CHAPTER 6

Behavioral Comparisons: Beyond the Surface

As I journey alongside my family-group, I've witnessed behaviors that resonate with similar human circumstances–bridging psychosis. These extend beyond superficial and into the realm of evolution's construction of emotions. Creating idiomatically contextual emotive structures that psychosomatically manifest homogeneously. I've learned that instincts are never "innate," and the importance of comprehending the inherent nature of societal dynamics and dependencies is inescapable within familial-species evolution.

For instance, the intricacies of trust. Humans learn to trust one another by establishing a healthy codependency through shared experiences, implied and assumed structures of coincident association, basic consistency, and the reliability of others. Dogs embark on exactly this same trust-building journey. We must comprehend familial dependency as an intrinsic obligation when deciding to be a cross-species human surrogate parent–an endeavor that transcends materialism.

Empathy bridges us, viscerally connecting on a profound level. Not confined to human hearts alone. Empathy is evolutionally structured in familial-species' biology. Dogs exhibit sentience enriched by sophisticated empathy relative to their rudimentary logic and emotive processing structures. Articulate communication, often viewed as the exclusive cornerstone of human interaction, is also present in all dogs. Their rich repertoire of body language serves as empirical guidance for the nuanced ability to convey thoughts and feelings. A tilt of the head or a wagging tail are not superficial assumptions–these are the threads of nonverbal language of authenticity and simplicity, which are <u>absolutely</u> quantifying.

Even as academia struggles to explore these complex behavioral parallels, it remains mindful of the distinct nature of each familial-specie. Dogs know we are not dogs. Dogs recognize that we literally control the majority of their life. Scientists must acknowledge and quantify these psychosomatic manifestations at the corresponding dilutive scale to enable the public to appreciate and honor the concrete evidence of sophisticated consciousness rather than dismissing anthropomorphism. The current mistakes birthed by academics anthropomorphizing their unfounded conjectures.

> *Don't anthropomorphize conjecture; anthropomorphize your intuition.*

The exploration of behavioral comparisons also leads us to reflect on the power of acceptance. Dogs appear to accept us without critical judgment. Yet, if a dog is afraid of you, that fear is the quantification of critical judgment. We must stop embodying their behavior generically as fearful or aggressive. "Unconditional love" is similarly wrong, as that defines a relationship of superficial infatuation.

> *"A dog is the only thing (sic) on earth that loves you more than you love yourself."*

This quote is attributed to Josh Billings, a pseudonym used by writer Henry Wheeler Shaw, who was from Monterey, California. His adage is naive. To love anything more than you love yourself is infatuation. It's disingenuous and quixotically naive. Anyone who loves you more than themself is insecure and becomes obsessive. High intradependency. We see this in human relationships around us. The adage treats trust, love, and familial dependencies without a foundation or emotional franchise conducive to building self-esteem in a cogent reciprocal structure. The apropos adage:

> *A dog is the only specie on earth that loves you as much as they love themself.*

That is cogent, healthy co/intra dependencies, reflecting critical self-objectification. Sophisticated biological life knows self-objectification. Let's recognize the shared emotions, intuitions, and social dynamics that unite us with dogs in profoundly isomorphic ways; a reminder we're all part of the intricate web of species consciousnesses–albeit a web woven with variegating threads of understanding, comprehension, empathy, and visceral connection. Our relationships with dogs give us insights into the evolution of consciousness itself, as well as the self-awareness of the depth of individual humanity. <u>Always</u> anthropomorphize your intuition.

Part 3
What We Need To Know

CHAPTER 7

Unveiling the Illusion: Media's Influence on Dog Behavior

Embarking on this chapter, I'm met with a profound awareness of the intricate web woven by the media–disaggregation with immense power to shape perceptions, often casting permanent *emotive* shadows of misconception for viewership. Delving into the influence of the media, I'm compelled to peel back at least one layer of misconception, shining a light on the truths that lie beneath.

Stereotypes and the Anatomy of Misinformation

Disconcerting facets of media influence are the perpetuation of breed stereotypes. Having witnessed this firsthand, I'm compelled to share my expertise. The story of the Pitbull, a breed enjoyably vilified by the media, is a poignant illustration. It's akin to judging an individual by their ethnicity, dismissing their unique identity in favor of lazy genericism stereotyping. My interactions with Pitbulls confirm the fallacy of breed stereotypes. Less than five percent of dangerous dogs are Pitbulls. The lower processing of lesser-humans is unable to "see the forest and the trees." It's analogous to saying, "all Chinese are bad drivers." It is a fallacy and a disservice to all dogs. There are no particular breeds that have uniquely evolved a predatory predilection. If Chihuahuas were 100 pounds, their infamy as angry and vicious would similarly apply. Dog bite websites are shrill, childish, deficient, grasping bunk. Dogs and humans are born predators.

Cogency exists within familial-species to enable sophisticated comprehension of one's environment, such as domestic structure. Dogs comprehend living in a home as a wholesale disingenuous experience. If an intact dog is abandoned in the wilderness, they will often survive and develop into a feral dog, which can circle back to their residential predation. Great Danes hunted and killed wild boars.[27]

[27] https://en.wikipedia.org/wiki/Great_Dane

A Journey Beyond the Façade

In this digital age, media is an omnipresent force–a medium amplifying the messages we receive. The portrayal of dog behavior is no exception. Beneath the glossy veneer of televised dog trainers and sensational headlines lies a world rife with ineptitude, misinformation, misrepresentation, and unchecked biases. There exists no show, trainer, or behaviorist who has a clue what they're talking about. The "dog whisperer" isn't real. A dog expert never uses training aids, never uses food, and never calls dogs "it." They never condone *behavioral euthanasia*, never turns down a predatory dog–regardless of whether the dog is 200 pounds or fifteen pounds–and the dog expert is 100 percent provably successful.

The media's portrayal of dog training and behaviorism reads as professional inexperience, leaving a trail of distorted perceptions in its wake, where the dysfunctional dog is killed. It's a lamentable truth that the media thrives on sensationalism. At the same time, the so-called dog expert goes home to cuddle their "normal" dog, which they often medicate. This derives from their need to qualify for prescribing medications to other families' dogs. They don't realize that their actions harm their own dog unnecessarily. Sometimes, they'll get a "normal dog" to center themselves–but the superficial quest for attention, ratings, viewership, and advertisers too often eclipses the pursuit of accuracy and genuine understanding of the world's most human-domesticated specie. Instead, this has led to the widening chasm between reality and the misconceptions propagated by both malicious and well-meaning, yet misinformed and inexperienced dog experts and academics.

You <u>are</u> your dog's *<u>safe harbor</u> for familial protection*. Your dysfunctional dog tries to cogently process without the benefit of an experienced, introspective structure. Objectification is functional.

Do Dogs Smell Fear?

Working alone with human-predatory giant dogs, scent is of no relevance and fails to entrench all aspects of behavior. Smelling "fear" is incidental. If you're hiking in the wilderness, confronted by a large predator twenty feet (six meters) from you, and you're downwind, your smell disperses behind you. The predator relies on visually comprehending your physical behavior–essentially quantifying your psychosomatic manifestations and noting disingenuous, unnatural movements. It's crucial to recognize that familial-species possess corresponding sophisticated biological cogency. Dogs behaving in dangerous manners are **not** lashing out; they're unable to process highly complex, foreign emotive structures that manifest psychosomatically. Dogs and familial-species navigate their world with a heightened sense of vulnerability in human regions.

Tail-tucking, lowered body posture, and changing gaze–these behaviors are consequential. Behaviors must be comprehended relative to the individual's personality, history, and circumstances–a chance for your anthropomorphic intuition to trust your instinct ("apex predator"). Movements are fundamentally designed for biologically articulable life yet remain functionally identical. These aren't simply gross expressions of "anxious" behavior.

The commonality of tail behavior in dogs, cats, lions, elephants, horses, monkeys, and other species is notable, as it stems from the evolutionary design and structure of consciousness in each specie. Tail behavior is destructured by musculature structure and fitness; rhythm, position (up, down, or midway), pattern (whether figure-8 or half-8), flicks, tucks, and physical cadence all carry meaning.

Ego: The Silent Saboteur of Progress

The role of ego–a formidable force retarding comprehension and growth. Many experts, propelled by the need to protect their reputations and bank accounts and uphold their image, are averse to admitting the limits of their knowledge. This systemic failure defines the existence of *behavioral euthanasia*. If someone is truly a dog expert, they <u>must</u> be able to rehabilitate ALL dysfunctional dogs.

Beyond the Buzzwords: *Behavioral Euthanasia*

Behavioral euthanasia conceals realities warranting scrutiny and full-throated criticism. Coined by academia, it reflects a profound lack of experience. I have yet to meet any dog who demonstrates self-loathing and self-hatred to be alive so as to desire suicide-by-human. In fact, dogs will fight **not** to be beaten despite lacking an idiomatic comprehension of death: themselves, and others. Capital punishment reflects the professional's malpractice, unethical shirking of personal responsibility, and truncated empathetic structure.

Behavioral euthanasia, once accepted without question, must be disproven for what it is: an academic attempt to sanitize the act of killing a dysfunctional dog. It's wholesale abhorrent, lacking empathetic effort to militate wanton killings. *Behavioral euthanasia* unanimously conveys the child on a tricycle with the front wheel missing, telling me why the sky is blue. It's a babbling bunk if the theory can't be proven in real life. Likewise, phrases such as "destroyed," "put down," and "put to sleep" are equally aghast labels for killing a dog.

Which is more difficult to accept:

A) six million dysfunctional dogs were killed last year

OR

B) six million dysfunctional dogs were euthanized last year.

Modern Science

This term is hubristic and deserves one simple response to destroy it. There exists absolutely no manner of "modern science" that can override the evolutionary construction of consciousness, also known as behavior. Behavior is psychological, not hungry. All dogs and humans are born predators.

Navigating Academia's White Labeling

Understanding "aggression" and all dysfunctions requires navigating away from using genericisms for the majority labeling of negative societal conduct. Terms such as "fear-based aggression," "medical aggression," "genetics," "reactive," "triggered," "dominance-based aggression," "breed," "age," and "some dogs are just born like that" reflect that the dog expert lacks expertise.

Dogs respond saliently via defensiveness to perceived threats. The fact is, all dogs cogently, logically, and emotionally think consequential of their immediate circumstance. If a "dangerous" dog isn't agitated, then no "reactivity" occurs. Yet categories such as "red zone," "bite level 6" and "severe psychological distress" are applied to dysfunctions that, on my scale, are only 3/10. This exhausting blame game, where dog experts blabber inanely with archaic phrases, has irrevocably damaged behaviorism.

"Aggression, reactive, and unpredictable" is secondary to *"flight, THEN fight."* The individual is simply trying to defend themselves, consequential to circumstance.

Take a human analogy: your sister keeps bugging you. You ask her to stop. If she stops, there will be no further conflict. If she bugs you again, you'll become more irritated, and you'll be forced to "react" consequential to her actions. For dogs, this is equitable. If you approach a dog that doesn't trust you or doesn't like you, and they bark angrily, lunges, or even bites, it's ignorance to blame them for your actions.

You literally control every aspect of your dog's life: going for walks, getting affection, when and what to eat, and providing clean water. If you show up three hours late to feed your dog, they aren't thinking, *"What a bad mom you are."* Your dog is thinking, *"OH MY GOSH, how did you know I was soooo hungry? You're amazing!!"*

This "structure of coincidence" psychologically bridges the relationship between how your dog is personally feeling and thinking, and how they interpret your presence and influence on their life. Remember, your dog can't do the physical things you can. Your dog communicates nonverbally with physical sophistication. Dogs actively introspect in relation to self-awareness and empathy.

This connotes the excitement of coming home. Just as a child in a big family is happy when they get to do an activity exclusively with their favorite parent, your dog will show and experience the same joy. To the inexperienced, this may appear as "dominant behavior," yet the excitement reflects familial-dependent cogency. Recognizing the distinctness in psychosomatic behavior paves the way for correct familial inclusion. Parental-predicated interactions teach dogs to comprehend emotionally congruent relationships.

The Neutering Myth Corrupts Behavioral Foundations

The notion that "neutering mitigates aggression" is a naive myth. I knew Nero was intact at ten years of age. I knew Andrew was intact at two years old. For an expert, hormones and genetics are insignificant. This relates to how pain is processed. Nurturing healthy behavioral foundations proves you understand nonverbal body language and verbal articulation. Nurture shapes behavior. Aggression due to chemical influences in the body again omits comprehending pain processing. Dog experts and doctors medicating dysfunctional dogs with strong psychopharmaceuticals have empirically disproven: Pharmaceutical-funded trimodal study spanning thirty-seven years concludes only fifteen percent efficacy of 83,388 clinically diagnosed participants.[28]

Nonverbal Communication, No Eye Contact

Dogs are keen observers of human behavior, especially when it comes to nonverbal communication. When your dog looks away while you're looking at them, it's not avoidance–it's nonverbal communication acknowledging mutual eye contact. Let's delve into the intricacies of exploring how dogs interpret human-specie nonverbal cues, and how this impacts mutual behavior. Correctly reviewing "silent dialogue" deepens our comprehension without human-specie insecurities. Debunking dogmatic posits: "Direct eye contact is uncomfortable, threatening to dogs." Eye contact isn't imperative, crucial, or fundamental communication. The ability to discern nuanced eye behavior and its physical manifestations in relation to the other party is profoundly crucial. Eye contact is deemed threatening by the inexperienced "dog expert." It's their inherent fear of being attacked, and their self-aware insecurity of ineptitude that conflates their inexperience with quantifying consciousness.

Both non-familial and familial-species psychosomatically manifest what they're thinking. This is due to a lack of rigid, articulated language, codependent societal structures, and the kind of fantastical abstraction humans often indulge in. Communication has never needed sustained direct eye contact. Direct eye contact is incidental–not primary, not even secondary. Exercising communication is more like being in love with someone speaking a different language: you feel before you fully understand.

Lack of bi-communication debilitates the dog expert. They fail to trust their own anthropomorphized intuition. Inexperienced dog experts panic at the thought of being killed or attacked, so they insist on eye contact to build tenuous bravado. Before the human-specie evolved oration, it read body language. Cognizably. The evolutional development of "talking" didn't occur instantly among early humans. During pre-Darwinian evolution, verbal communication–and the subsequent hereditary comprehension of receptiveness in the listener–caused both instinct and intuition to

[28] http://bit.ly/41XGGJH

become lethargic, resulting in higher taxation toward the development of sophisticated human consciousness. Random early human listeners within regions would defaultively be introspectively confused by the clouded cogency of what they heard, coupled with the speaker's physical actions, which are commensurate with the *speaker's* verbalization. Over a very long time, a contextually complex interpretation evolved within the human brain's structural homogeneity, allowing primal cogency to abstract "language" to psychologically establish, emerging across evolutionary time due to the rigidity of idiomatic contextualization

As evolution progresses, each iterative listening would tenuously comprehend the bi-communication occurring and *may* attempt to self-discover how to reply–initiating or continuing monosyllabic or recitative conversation–while others in the social family-group may or may not be able to comprehend or concentrate their own bodies to verbalize physically. Newborn children, in particular, would be the first to attempt a primal, instinctive understanding of deliberate communication. Yet their human parents–whether temporary, transitory, or transient–might not comprehend that the child's sounds are deliberate efforts to communicate with them. Cognizance is not going to be instantaneous; the chicken-or-egg scenario is an evolutionary logic.

Primary communication has always been nonverbal. Your intuition is predicated upon your instinct, which is in turn predicated upon your apex predator to cognitively discern body language observed, cogently surmise, and conclude that the physical or verbal behavior is deliberately or objectively directed. Nonverbal communication plays a significant role in the development of empathy. It's a residential construction, and a function of introvertive self-objectification.

Body language is omnidirectional, as observed by all third parties with line of sight. Consider this analogy: you're sitting beside your romantic partner, watching a movie. A few minutes earlier, you had a small argument. While watching, you reach over to hold their hand, and they pull it away. A few more minutes pass, you try again; once more, they pull it away. On the third attempt, they finally turn and say, "Can't you see that I don't want to hold hands? That's why I keep pulling away."

You knew the message the first time. Despite an overt and obtuse display, this nonverbal communication is evident to all observers.

A dog's verbalization is the last resort for communication. Aggregate every sound your dog makes in twenty-four hours: barks, woofs, and whines. Your dog's verbalization collectively adds up to less than two minutes. That represents 99.7 percent of nonverbal communication is physical nuance and psychosomatic manifestation. Equally representative is how early humans began to "talk." The necessity to discuss relates to the emotive and psychological cogency of cause and effect. Despite the human-specie having sophisticated consciousness, the relevance of communication must be important, effective, ego-centric, and emotionally relevant. Dogs are not verbalizing for socially collective aggrandizement but to physically express psychological ideation. Although verbalization is socially dependent, sustaining communication isn't required due to the lack of socio-engineering complexity. There is no requisite to over-talk.

Hence, eye contact is a form of incongruent communication. If a dog expert advises dog parents to make their dog maintain eye contact, it explicitly proves they don't comprehend subtle nonverbal communication, and this further denigrates healthy familial-inclusive relationships, assuring dysfunction affecting self-esteem and self-worth.

Despite academia assuming that killing dogs is demarcated by the degree of "psychological distress," extremely traumatized dogs are ***fulsomely*–100 percent–**rehabilitable. Take Mingki, a Jindo born into a horrific, deplorable South Korean meatdog farm and rescued at just a year and a half. In South Korea, "ripe meatdogs" are considered most desirable once they reach two years of age.

Mingki's story illustrates that self-awareness is an evolution foundate for sophisticated consciousness and is constructionally fundamental for objective emotive communication. After more than a year after rescue, Mingki heard the voice of his rescuer–the woman who had spent that entire year pleading with the meatdog farm owner for his release. Mingki recognized her voice immediately. His affection of interest motivated by introspective processing of historical comparative.[29]

Language is the regional-psychological compartmentalization of a wholesale societal manifestation of mostly similar cogencies across all

[29] Arf Arf Bark Bark Rescue & Rehab, "Skittish, Biting Rescue Dog Mingki #4 - Animal Hope and Wellness Foundation," *YouTube*, posted June 19, 2018, https://www.youtube.com/watch?v=sUTHwTtG_I8&t=281s

iteratives of any familial-specie–verbalization produced from introspected, ego-selfish desire. At first, it is involuntary, such as falling down and the body responding, causing sound and psychosomatic manifestations. Then, it becomes deliberate, furthering one's emotional and social interdependency progressively, and by default, through objective forced self-awareness (introspective) to which evolution structurally creates "morality" with language. Objectively, from empatheticism: the emotional desire to share in a like-minded manner.

In other words, early humans emotionally expressed their rudimentary emotions, both psychologically and directly, causing their bodies to vocalize in response to another early human or animal as a form of communication. This is the first signal of deliberate consciousness objectification: gauging sentient targets within the development of its empathetic structure.

The development of communicative languages is a process of emotive compartmentalization, psychologically influenced by societal history, region, and environment. Evolutionary cognitive sophistication in constructing grammatical dialects or languages is predicated upon the taxonomic psychological syntax of the regional grouping of the familial-specie(s).

Complex articulation is need-only–early human comprehension of socialness and commonness by naming items through the mutual creation of a lingua-franca, i.e., "words." Self-awareness of sounds coming from the body of early humans is recognized introspectively and became learnable and controllable. Early humans who ran and fell would produce a force-constricted exhalation, a "sound" in response to the impact or injury. Over time, this default response evolved into an introspective structure: *"why and how did I make that sound?"*

Flatulence, burping, ligaments or popping joints or knuckles–hearing sounds coming from one's physical self requires complex-to-sophisticated consciousness to conclude as cause-and-effect–along with the aptitude to recreate sound deliberately. The sound of falling and suffering, evoking pain, required complex early humans to introspectively possess complex emotive motivation to self-entertain by recreating the same sound–an egocentric quest to determine if others could congruently express similar primal talents. The shared commonality of sound would be perceived as incidental, anecdotal, and involuntary rather than deliberate communication. From this, the evolutionary creation of language unfolded: first monosyllabic sounds, then tonal variation, then the musicality of tone, eventually leading to multi-syllabic sounds.

Language and communication: the context of words and grammar structures socially-regionalized containment, attaching emotional pertinence to language constructively. For example, a neighborhood is often referred to as having a unique character, or "vibe," due to its social and emotional aspects.

Humans often assign different definitions to the same psychological act despite using the same language. For example, to *lie* is to *prevaricate*; to prevaricate is to lie—and all the synonyms in between. The act of "lying" is psychological. Yet, linguistically, definitions are verbosely descriptive due to the contextual restraint (social politeness) of language. These contribute to the arrangement of words grammatically for syntactic flow.

Take another analogy: you receive a text from someone's spouse, and you can't figure out if they're being serious or making a joke. You ask their partner about the text, and they say, *"Oh, she's just joking; that's her sense of humor."*

Dogs and children can't self-actualize, especially when dealing with complex, foreign emotions without healthy idiomatic, logical, introspective, and familiarity with historical comparatives. The difficulty of complex emotives for dogs is that another dog can't say to your dog "woof woof" to effectively bi-communicate what your dog is introvertedly feeling and explain why they feel as they do. Human surrogate parenting provides a context that develops a dog's or child's self-objectification, also known as introspective structuring, within a safe harbor.

Illuminating the Path Forward

As I navigate these complexities, a vision of transformation emerges—a path transcending the media's misrepresentations, ego-driven agendas, and unjustifiable practices. It is a path that leads us to the core of what it means: clarifying and delving into a new realm—exploring consciousness in the context of evolution. It requires us to question, unlearn, and seek the truth beyond the media's shadows. We stand poised to illuminate our paths forward. You're now embarking on a journey that is empirically superior to the collective knowledge of behavior and consciousness gathered by all *the planet's universities*.

Part 4
Why Dogs Act the Way They Do

CHAPTER 8

"Aggression" Beyond Genericism

My journey explains the aggregate nature that foundates aggression in various contexts and implications. It's with compassion and deep insight that I express opposition to genericism, such as using terms like "aggression" and "genetics" to describe what is fundamentally not generic.

The Genetic and Nurturing Dance: Nature *and* Nurture

Behavior in dogs is not two-dimensional but rather a symphonic composition where nature and nurture play primary roles, timelessly influencing residential-psychological emotive predispositions. Healthily nurturing dependencies benefits healthy behavioral upbringing wielding emotive gravitas. Dogs' behavioral expressions are not permanently hardwired; they're shaped through experiences, interactions, and the external guidance that we, as human surrogate parents, provide. The environment is the nurture, which is the primary influence over nature, in slivers *within* the tenths of a second. Behavior is consciousness, not delineations. Comprehending consciousness means there is no dualistic analog choice, as that implies parallel processing to be decisively chosen, which is paradoxical, much like a child unable to decide amidst a vibrant flow of thought.

Realizing that the domestication of any animal is disingenuous to all species except humans. There are no finely engineered mathematically dependent structures outside the human-specie. If an intact dog whose heredity has generationally been domesticated is banished far into the wilderness to live with other wild dogs and procreates, within three generations, domesticate traits would be diluted and bred out. Fourth-generation offspring would be considered wholly feral—a true wild dog. If we capture and bring that fourth-generation dog to an experienced adopter, habilitation and domestication are 100 percent doable. Accommodation is readily comprehended by that dog, and they'll become emotionally stable and domestically enriched members through human parenting. This is not human-conducted accommodation but rather represents the dog specie's evolutionary existing competence to emotionally and psychologically understand their domestic structure as part of intimate cross-species cohabitation. With a human apex predator in familial disingenuity. Emotive isomorphism.

In many countries, wild feral dogs, such as the Formosan Mountain Dog on the island of Taiwan, are routinely trapped by dog rescuers and successfully adopted by families. These are irrefutable debunkings of "genetics."

The intelligence to comprehend one's environment is rooted in the sophistication structure of consciousness, specie-relative at the corresponding dilutive scale. The permanent retardation in academia is a result of both collective and individual inexperience, leading to miscomprehension and academic stagnation. Selectively curating for research reflects the low level of research competency. All dogs, like humans, are born with a predatory instinct. Dogs don't have malicious, fantastical ideations and egos selfishly predilected. Nurture is inter/co/intra dependencies.

The fundamental discourse is that academia has historically lacked real-world experience, resulting in systemic resistance to acknowledging its ineptitude. It's normal for behaviorists to be abjectly scared of being viciously attacked or killed by a dysfunctional dog. When one lacks the comprehension to recognize psychological behavior as emotive dysfunctions, the outward psychosomatic manifestations are far over their heads. And typically viewed two-dimensionally by PhD behaviorists as "hopeless," whose own safety fears, defensively dead ends thus enacting academic flight; thus, PhDs deem dysfunctional dogs: "unfixable." Nature inherently influences individual variations of personality. Claims of selectively domesticating dogs are not a discretionary victory for us. It's anecdotal and ignorant. Failing comprehension of the emotive elicitation of nonhuman species' familial evolution relies on the preexisting structure of consciousness that has endured through emotional isomorphism, establishing familial relationships much further back than 30,000 years.

The following cases illustrate how nurture can profoundly shape a dog's behavior, often exceeding the influence of genetics or early environment.

- **Nurture exceeds nature, circumstance, environment:** Gordon the dangerous, disabled Bulldog diagnosed with Dandy Walker Syndrome.[30]

[30] Arf Arf Bark Bark Rescue & Rehab, "Dangerous Disabled and Reactive Puppy (Gordon the Bulldog)," *YouTube*, posted July 3, 2019, https://www.youtube.com/watch?v=D0LzlxLnXNY/

- **Nature and nurture:** Cody the Jindo from a "meatdog" farm with dissimilar dysfunctions relative to Mingki.[31]
- **Nature and nurture:** Mingki, the Jindo "meatdog" born and raised on a South Korean "meatdog" farm.[32]
- **Nurture exceeds nature and initial nurture environment:** George the Spitz from family home to tied outdoors for two years.[33]
- **Nature and nurture adjusted:** Axel the German Shepherd from happy puppy to dangerous adult.[34]

How Do Dogs Assess for Threats?

Assessing threats without words–through physical gait structure, maturation of physical behavior (such as if the age of the subject is unknown, the observer can ascertain whether the subject is young or old; we can see, when a small person walks, if they are a child, young adult, or have dwarfism, etc.), posture–comes as intuitively as "smelling fear." Field-of-vision processing for sighted individuals evaluates redundant and rhetorical movements, such as full-foliage branches moving within the wind's range versus prey that cause disingenuous movement within the redundancy.

Dogs employ a multi-sensory approach to evaluating potential threats. With their remarkable ability to smell, hear, see, and taste, dogs gather information about their surroundings. A scenario involved Sammie when without warning came fast-approaching Walter and Lincoln Jr. toward her, illustrates this process. Sammie, vigilant due to her tiny size and disability, watched them closely as they approached her–observing their behavior, listening for adversarial sounds, and making eye contact with both to determine individual intent. Sammie gauges intent by the manner of each individual's physical gait, whether it is a natural expression of personality or a disingenuous one. In the intricacy of sensory perception, logic, and cogent dwelling on her emotions–which would typically cause heightened

---

[31] Arf Arf Bark Bark Rescue & Rehab, "Skittish Dog: Cody the Jindo from Nami Kim. Trainers/Behaviorists Over 2.5 Years Couldn't Downtrain," *YouTube*, posted April 8, 2020, https://www.youtube.com/watch?v=zDOyMMO00aY

[32] Arf Arf Bark Bark Rescue & Rehab, "Mingki from Animal Hope and Wellness Foundation," *YouTube, https://www.youtube.com/playlist?list=PLK43vpl6h3zZHdeWx-KPdes5gKdXaf6CM.*

[33] Arf Arf Bark Bark Rescue & Rehab, "Dangerous Feral Dog Attacks - George's FULL STORY," *YouTube,* posted March 20, 2018, https://www.youtube.com/watch?v=CZVdctLZWw4

[34] Arf Arf Bark Bark Rescue & Rehab, "DANGEROUS DOG - German Shepard Bites People, Attacks Other Dogs," *YouTube,* posted July 19, 2018, https://www.youtube.com/watch?v=laGKEyiNHJ0

self-awareness–familial-species employ extremely efficient discernment of comparative, rhetorical, and redundant processes more so than just utilizing evolutionarily efficient skills.

Sammie's assessment of threats, to decide whether to engage or maintain peaceful coexistence, involves comprehending that Sammie doesn't need to escape via flight nor feel cornered to the point where she feels escape (flight/defense) is improbable or impossible, and thus be forced into fighting due to being defenseless, if she concludes she failed to do so initially.

Here's another analogy: your partner walks up to you in a highly subtle, nuanced manner that feels odd, causing you to sense intuitively that something is off. You recognize your partner's current physical gait behavior against your memory-comparative large mapping model of them, which represents their psychosomatic-physiological personality as a flow of nonverbal communication.

Each familial-specie when separated into its taxonomy has a commonly shared physical movement flow–a natural flavor and style of movement. Just as language is a regional manifestation, compartmentalized of localized societal psychology, physical behavior will share similarities in such specie's nuance.

For instance, as you watch a crowd of people walking, you *will* notice one of them walking with a slight limp. Your recognition of crowd flow and anomalies, or dysfunction, through unnatural behavior by any individual is an identifiable variant. You note them individually. From such notice, you identify, both aggregatively and dis-aggregatively, what you see and know about "how humans walk."

Note that the functions of threat assessment are closely tied to how dogs and animals and humans process their field of vision. Noticing a gate swinging open and close in the wind is, firstly, a unique rhetorical device against the known movements (behavior) of the gate, which is typically closed (redundant). As the gate continues to swing, the movement is considered redundant in itself due to the observing individual's cogent familiarity with the gate's behavior. It's erroneous for the academe to create separate or multiple decision-making complexes, such as modalities of consciousness, which would cause greater biological robustness within the areas of functional and contributory consciousness.

Simple Threats

The first time your rescue dog sees you come out of the shower, they may panic because they cannot yet physically recognize you, though they recognize your voice. The incongruency is analogous to your friend dressing up in disguise. This can happen to some rescue dogs, as they're not familiar with your (geometric) physical appearance and may run away in panic, become angry, or appear menacing toward you.

There's a cogent decision between "I thought it was you!" and "Who are you, stranger and why do you sound so familiar?" that must be made; at the same time, an emotional attachment is intensively introspecting: "Am I at risk?" This is predicated upon redundant and rhetorical mannerisms evolutionally comprehended as the groundwork for consciousness' quickness of efficiency.

Such as going outside: here's why your dog may start barking. Your dog's sense of safety when going into your backyard means that barking is a way to preemptively alert potential threats that your dog is entering into an area of unknown safety, alone. This stems entirely from a fear of unknown threats and is rooted in "what's unknown, and what I can't see," especially at night.

Barking may seem boisterous. Still, it's most often threat-preventative–alerting and announcing to possible, potential live threats (complex fantastical ideation) that your dog introvertively comprehends. This predicates marginalization, abandonment, and introspective impairment. Conversely, when you and your dog are going for a walk, stepping outside your front door typically doesn't cause your dog to bark. The protection of the leash is supported by your physical hold, supporting your familial (cogency of) protection by holding the leash.

Listen to how your dog barks: repetitive natures recur in their verbalization. You will hear your dog's own VoiceKey (intonation, inflection, rhythm, etc.), despite seeming nonsensical or without rhyme or reason. Carefully listening will avail barking tones that are deliberate acts of contextualizing intelligence of consciousness. Language isn't truncated as with humans.

The structure functionally assessing threats encompasses a myriad of circumstances to gauge and scale from, and within. The process of academia's threat assessment for a dog often unfolds in a systematic manner due to the pedestrian manner of life and incestuous lineal education.[35]

Nurturing Puppies, Early Intervention, and the Specious "Fear Periods"

Its pedantic miscomprehension of "fear periods" exists in young dogs' development. It's mis-categorizing highly contextualized nuances of psychological develing and egoist self-awareness. As dogs age, their emotive comprehension develops along with cognition. These two conflate, yet are constantly at different stages of maturation, resulting in incongruency of cogency. Inexperience is wrongly concluded as demarcative. As puppies grow into teenhood, there are domestic shifts at home. The adoration of a new puppy wears off, causing less attention, and the relationship ages, eventually leading to a decline. Too big, too hyper, and too clingy during aging, their dog causes humans to pull back relationally.

Dogs require context to process their uncouth emotive structures. Their life circumstances are the idiomatic context. Reset-hugs provide a sense of commonality, a safe harbor, and a sense of familial dependency. Psychological develing occurs literally each second, compositing all circumstances into functional constructs, relative to individual personality. Consistent parenting reduces the potential for adverse interactions before they can psychologically shape puppyhood and beyond. The playfulness, anger, frustration, and other emotional expressions that dogs exhibit are unique to an individual's immediate circumstances.

Interpretation of circumstances, rudimentary societal behaviors, introspective weighting, and inter-relational communication, including biting, can be evaluated by comprehending that transitional discernment stages are **not** "fear periods." Stereotyping obligates bias interpretation. Expecting dogs to conform to misguided stereotypic conduct, expression, and generalizations results in affixing prejudicial labels of misbehavior.

---

[35] The use of "incestuous lineal education" is to spotlight the academic in-breeding of knowledge. This phrase is not meant to distract but to describe the manner which behaviorism, and associated studies, demands with incessance that all proposed theories be reliant upon previous academic works peer-reviewed. My work is untouchable and empirical theorem due to the entire absence of behaviorism.

Recognizing developing traits as aggregatively conflational, juvenile consciousness transitions toward adulthood in real time. Interactions must be intuitively anthropomorphized, discerning regular play and comprehending potential fights; they aren't compartmentalized.

Cultivating coextensive emotive-isomorphism maturation relative to familial contextualized structure—as dog and parent—through sustaining familial protection allows for idiomatic contextualization at your dog's level of cogency.

Experts struggle to comprehend how dogs process their rudimentary logic and emotional processing structures. Behavior exists at scale as context-relative. Consciousness relies upon evolution's shared biological "engineering schematic" for construction. Emotions aren't a self-regulating mechanism independently realized. Familial-species, including human, can't self-actualize or self-soothe in highly complex, foreign emotive circumstances due to a lack of indigenous familiarity.

Humans are physically tall giants, regardless of dogs' quickness and powerful attributes. Dogs defend themselves primarily with their mouths. Unable to trust their human parent to familially protect them, your dog concludes that they must protect themselves, given their limited options.

In the case of strangers, dogs would think, *"Why is the stranger walking towards us—and then me?"* The stranger is an immediate physical context. The erroneous technique is to "turn direction and leave" or pull to the side as the stranger passes. These prove to your dog that you can't protect them; instead, they perceive you are running away. Your dog's belief and faith that you're protecting them is *their* most urgent perspective. *"My giant, powerful mom can't recognize I'm scared of the stranger, and we 'run away'";* your dog learns you will not and cannot protect them. Dogs, processing minutiae, begin to denigrate their own self-confidence and relevance within your family on a rudimentary foundation.

This is akin to toddlers who are afraid of big, imposing adults they don't know—like when you were a child approaching an imposing adult or staying with an aunt you were scared of, being alone with them and defenseless to escape.

Another example can be seen in videos where their dog is home alone, sleeping, and a burglar breaks in. Their dog barks, growls, lunges, or even tries to bite. But if the burglar is dog-savvy, acts friendly, and engages in play, soon, their dog ends up playing with the burglar.

Aggressive training methods tacitly oppress and subjugate, retarding your dog's need for the safety of what they're seeing and feeling. Approaches based on dominance, "alpha," or "leader" literally sow fear, impose psychological mistrust, and render above-average intelligent dogs subjugated, wary, and trepidatious of humans while truncating cogency. This will cause complex emotives to propagate previously manageable traits into debilitating dysfunction, comprising structures of jealousy, abandonment, low self-esteem, and low self-worth. Oppressive methods impact dogs' social comprehension.

Field-of-Vision Processing

Consciousness first evolved with the simple sensations–such as the warmth of the sun felt by sightless biological structures–and develops into a deliberate affection for warmth. Though dogs have less sophisticated eyes, the consideration is how efficiently vision is processed.

Live motion is actually a series of infinitesimal frames of vision. Redundant and rhetoric processing allows for interpretation of "what's different between this image and the immediately preceding image." The brain's ability to process minuscule mismatching of nearly identical images of 2D frames per eye. Stereoscopic sight must be confluent while calibrating with the body's other sensory and psychological inputs.

Tracking a hidden figure begins with detecting tiny visual cues–a sliver of movement within the image. Field-of-vision processes it into hyper-short-term memory for redundancy comparison to identify sequential discrepancies. Consciousness identifies the rhetorical movement of what's already known, determining anomalies within the field of vision: *is there something moving out-of-ordinary known motions? Is it the shape, pattern, and color?* Vision processes geometrically topographic, gauging influences such as the natural range of motion.

The computational brain power processed very slowly and required a physically stable environment, as "intelligent quickness" was primordial. There was no instant vision comprehension. Images began to reveal a difference between dark-to-bright transitions, then blurred dynamic depth, to the entire field of vision evolutionarily learning the macro. The "blur" is identified as mobility evolved, allowing for physical inspection, thus evolving a comprehensive definition of vision. Evolution didn't linearly create eyesight, which contrasts with the artificial intelligence pixel-based approach.

Managing Quick Emotional Transitions

There is a common yet misguided belief that "dogs are unpredictable," as if shifting suddenly from joy to anger without reason. Often, it's due to an emotional feeling rather than a trait or dysfunction of self-marginalization, without seeming to reflect or represent any provocation or predicate. This dogma overlooks the fact that dogs physically process significant information of their immediate circumstance at a rate faster than five-hundredths of a second (1/20), considering that Bruce Lee was able to reactively press a button in conjunction with a light flash within two-tenths of a second (2/10). The emotive structure of dogs is processed extremely quickly and with less complex ideation.

The key is that behavior isn't a sustained plateau in any specie's complexity and isn't simplistic. Dysfunctional dogs don't "regress," they cognitively plateau. There is always an emotional and psychological cause for transition. Just as the misnomer dogs are "reactive" when, factually, dogs behave consequentially. *Thinking* is influenced by the circumstances and individuals involved.

It takes time and patience to downtrain, stabilize, and rehabilitate any dog deemed a human predator, extremely dangerous, or extremely vicious into a rehabilitated, self-confident individual. Dog experts are so scared; they lack the intuition or intelligence to withstand their abject fears, coupled with the urgent, real-time demand against their inexperience, which makes them erroneously think dogs are "reactive and unpredictable."

This process requires an understanding of your dog's circumstances and consequent behaviors through empathetic objectification. Trusting your intuition anthropomorphically, you'll help your dog's emotional health find cogency-evolving ways to cope with their prior abuse, trauma, abandonment, and all the very horrible emotions that cause your dog to default–instead of ignorantly concluding *behavioral euthanasia.*

The Cogency of Gravity, a.k.a. Physics

The problem currently in the public square is the tacit expectation that dogs show us overtly, blatant signs of communication and "thinking consciousnessly." The fact that familial-species are literally presenting obtuse communication is a perpetual shame for academia to be missing and comprehending how dogs and animals *constantly* naturally communicate via body behavior, essentially developing physical personality, a.k.a. predictable body gait behavior, and homogeneous-familiar movements. All overtly determinable as homogenous to the familial-specie(s) being studied: the manner of communicating doesn't require sophisticated or complex bi-communication; hence, body language *is* omnidirectional and comprehensible by all direct line-of-sight viewers. Body language expresses overt functions of "thinking"; this is obtuse.

Dogs comprehend how things move and fall, and if there is a trajectory, not just straight lines, such as when something drops and how it naturally falls straight to the ground. How the object angles/arches during its movement. *Velocity targeting* reflects the brain's ability to comprehend the natural mathematical pattern of motion within a specific context of movement. This is essentially processing "physics" in an animalistic, rather than mathematical, manner. There's no wonder, but instead, a comprehension of simplicity. Walking over a suspension bridge with a see-through metal grate walkway causes grave concern for many dogs because the ground below can be seen through the grate, which suggests that the steel walkway will not be strong enough to support their weight. This fear is commonly enacted by tourists walking on glass bridges.[36]

Life's aggregate knowledge of weight-bearing structures *is* recalled relative to prior circumstances–where similar appearing structures or dimensions have or haven't supported the individual's weight. These are memories that serve as *idiomatic contextualizations of historical comparatives*. For example, stepping on a thin stick and feeling it snap informs future judgments about similar objects. This demonstrates that dogs rely on long-term memory which is a required trait of sophisticated emotive consciousness. Trauma impairs, aided by endurance.

---

[36] CGTN, "Tourist terrified by new glass walkway that cracks under weight," *YouTube*, posted October 10, 2017, https://www.youtube.com/watch?v=Oo0NJsr5m4I.

Dogs have limited introspective application of physics when living in a home. Mnemonic comprehension of the grate's appearance contextually conveys that the bridge can't support weight when walking on it: *"If I walk on this flimsy bridge, it will fail, and I will fall."* Hence, physics is purely utilitarian, whereas mathematic and engineering are anthropomorphically very important to the human-specie. Your dog's refusal to cross a flimsy-*looking* structure is pure cogency. Dogs process consciousness viscerally. Complex emotionality allows for a logically functional and introspective individual of their specie, to cogently analyze and conclude based on known facts, historical comparisons, and their level of cognitive and emotional maturity. Your dog's refusal to walk across is a valid logical conclusion based on their life's known facts and similar historical experiences, and it is the same manner in which the human-specie functions.

Here's an analogy: you're cutting meat to freeze, and your dog watches with egotistic attention waiting to see whether you'll give some to them or if a piece will fall to the floor. As you drop pieces into the freezer bag, one misses and lands on the counter. Your dog anticipates and tracks it as though it had fallen to the floor–you can see their head and eyes following the piece from your hand to the bag, to the counter, and then toward the floor. This shows fantastical ideation at work. The second and subsequent times a piece misses the bag, your dog may glance downward toward the floor despite concluding that the second piece is likely also on the countertop. Repeat this a third time, and your dog won't look at the floor unless there is a change in your physical movement or the emotional circumstance, such as a shift in your VoiceKey indicating a piece is for them. The subsequent circumstances demonstrate cogency.

Everything is about Trust. Consider this trust analogy: you are on a work trip with a newly hired coworker who seems sketchy, and you have to share a hotel room with them. Naturally, you will hide your valuables and wallet, guard your passwords with extreme caution. You'll also be cautious about what you talk about and how you talk, so as to protect your personal information–your *"self."*

Understanding Emotions and Context: Psychosomatic Manifestations

The crux of dysfunctional behavior is destructuring and disaggregating emotive contextualization. Familial-species such as dogs and humans have intricate emotional landscapes, experiencing a plethora of emotions at a correspondingly diluted scale, relative to the sophisticated consciousness of humans, given their biological complexity. Animals don't need linear academic pursuits or self-obsessive, superficial introspection. Familial-species don't need self-gain fantastical ideation. Behavior is consciousness, not a standalone, consecutive, or concurrent phenomenon. It is the functioning abstraction of aggregating structures that conflate within the individual's psychological introspection and objectification–the constant neuronic flow for idiomatic ideation.

Emotive structures are extremely nuanced, comprising individual neuronic flows that proceed in upwards of hundreds of millions of journeying pathways at any given time. Each electrical iteration proceeds independently, yet together they create the effect of a "Ghost in the Machine"–a sheer volume of directioned electrical flows.

Imagine a snowstorm: each snowflake crystallizes and falls at different times, colliding along established tendrils of airflow. Influenced by the environment. Snowflakes consequentially merge, though the majority maintain independent (single iterative) journeys. The resistive yet agreeable nature of neurotubules enables exponential flows. Electrical resistivity depends on the brain's neurological robustness, while electrical frequency creates a kind of "callusing," smoothing each neurotubule's biological construct.

Behavior is entirely consequential and circumstantial, regardless of the environment, and is influenced by both nature and nurture. When attempting to quell "aggression," we must look beyond the surface of emotional and physical manifestations to the deeper factors influencing human or animal actions. This requires abandoning genericism labels, which prejudicially declare antisocial and negative behaviors as "innate." It's imperative to acknowledge the permafrost built by academia's centuries of miscomprehensions, which continue to compound academia's chronicle of failures in comprehending consciousness. Consciousness isn't "innate" nor unfathomable. Through the lens of compassion and common sense, "aggression" is a harmful reflection of academic blindness ad infinitum.

The Soul of a Dog: Destructuring Behavior and the Construct of Consciousness is a theorem–rooted in the basic mathematical conduct of biology, yet focused primarily on the abstractive evolution of consciousness. Behavior isn't a standalone trait caused by mysterious or divine influence, but relatively a simple Boolean logic of cause-and-effect at the most basic function of "neurotubules mathematic."

Evolution stems from the proof of the schematic of the "first cells" as a common ancestor. Yet it has been erroneously misinterpreted by human arrogance, which demarcates consciousness. This inefficiency, contrary to all standards of biological logic, miscomprehends evolution's economy and thus forgets the obligation for the superiority of a single biological engineering schematic. The causation of consciousness was unavoidable due to aggregating mathematical conflation, requiring a default trifecta of emotive structures to create illogic that flowed simultaneously with logic within the same time segments.

Nurturing healthy familial bonds based on implicit trust, employing idiomatically relevant and familial contextualized structures, and recognizing the importance of consistent and early intervention are strategies to unravel misconceptions that lead academia astray. Aside from the chronic defaulting to "killing the dysfunctional dog," the most extremely predatory dogs, such as Nero and Walter, have all been rehabilitated using my simple parenting protocols.

Stabilizing dysfunctional dogs on their path to emotional harmony begins by understanding that dogs don't automatically recognize their highly complex emotions or know how to contextualize them idiomatically without prior historical comparative reference. The critical role here is to provide a safe harbor—a protective familial environment that ensures the dog parent's protection is consistently reliable. Much like patiently teaching an angry child to self-regulate instead of distracting it (the child) with a toy or treat, dogs similarly can learn to calm themselves through the safety provided by their human surrogate parent by establishing familial protection thereby offsetting natural default to extreme emotives of rage or joy.

CHAPTER 9

Navigating Dysfunctions: Compassion as Our North Star

Delving deeper into the intricacies and confusions within the public sphere, the phrase "canine fear-based aggression" draws attention to one of its most poignant threads, which needs unraveling: the myopic attribution of dysfunctional dogs exhibiting negative behaviors as "fear-based aggression." Ironically, this precedent label reflects abject systemic miscomprehension by **all experts**. Miscomprehensions of academe failed for centuries to correlate consciousness existing in all familial-species.

Behaviors are psychological and bridgeable relative to human psychosis. Self-awareness exists in moderate-to-sophisticated species. Extremes such as human predation can be stabilized. It's not "addressing impulses" but teaching a sophisticated sentient specie to "pause and think" emotionally rather than assuming a very limited emotionality. Cohabitating familially with another apex specie debunks "flight or fight." Cohabitation relies on emotively introverted dependency to cogently conclude a personal interest in domestication.

Labeling dogs "fearful" only justifies academia's lack of validity in rehabilitating dysfunctional dogs' behaviors. Professional malpractice in killing dysfunctional dogs *proves* to lack the depth of an empathetic heart, failing comprehensively functional perspective due to the inability to recognize psychosomatic manifestations and quantifications of consciousness.

Failure to detail the disaggregates of dysfunctions always leads to declaring dysfunctional dogs as "severely psychologically distressed," a typical precursor inexperienced behaviorists claim when killing dysfunctional dogs. Seeking navigation of tumultuous waters by declaratory "fear-based aggression," yet for behaviorists believing themselves "experts" must refuse to condone *behavioral euthanasia*. It's imperative to escape the chain of hubristic academia.

Fear: Erroneously Espoused as Primary Root

What does the academia think causes fear? Why don't they talk about the cause? "Fear" is their blanket, restrictively kneecapping, as with "innate." The expert who has stopped following their intuitive logic processing, therefore, retarding their intelligence of destructuring and disaggregating behavior, ergo consciousness. Fear stems from a sense of unprotection and abandonment, regardless of whether dog, lion or human. Defenselessness and insecurity are born. These answers the fundamental questions: "How *can* insecurities develop?" or "What needs to exist for insecurities to also exist?"

Fear is far more complex. It comes from any emotion, especially love. Fear of losing love is to lose protection and be introvertively-aware of abandonment. Feeling unsafe and alone, from introspective into introvertive, predicates upon emotive erosion–the unhealthy structure of familial protection. Who can a scared dog trust if their parent doesn't acknowledge their concerns for personal safety? Fear is not a genericity of emotive structures. "Consciousness" is a biological, psychological, and wholesale emotive structure. Human parents not consistently acknowledging and validating their dog's or child's lucid interpretation of their immediate circumstances demonstrate to their ward a profound abdication of their obliged human (surrogate) parenting protection.

Stockholm syndrome is a proposed condition or theory that tries to explain why hostages sometimes develop a psychological bond with their captors.[37]

Your inherently deep emotional dependency on your dog literally controls every aspect of your relationship with them, whether it be going for a walk, a car ride, toys, and games, or even the time of their death. Humans are, by nature, inherently more powerful and larger than dogs. An eight-year-old child stands taller than a Great Dane. The human ability to concisely talk and move in amazing ways; your dog comprehends the veil of intradependency that is familial and parental.

Remember when you believed your dad was the smartest in the world? Over time, you learned he wasn't as smart as you'd thought. If you don't ingenuously acknowledge your dog's emotions relative to dysfunctional manifestations, forcing your dog to believe their parent isn't watching and protecting them will force your dog's self-defense. You consistently "know

---

[37] https://en.wikipedia.org/wiki/Stockholm_syndrome

everything about them, and care about what they do," yet when your dog feels scared, they need and expect you to acknowledge, proving you're protective. Otherwise, you effectively reduce the trust your dog has in you. Instead of showing your dog why they need you, you're **not** there. This may comprise just one percent of daily concerns, but this is how global structures of dependencies degrade. Your dog's self-esteem suffers when they witness their human parent failing to acknowledge dire circumstances for them. When your dog consciousnessly experiences no security from the real world, they will conclude that you don't know how to protect them, and you have abandoned them when they needed you the most.

Trust is when you go to lunch with a friend, and when they forget their wallet, you lend them $20. A week passes, and your friend still hasn't paid you back. Three weeks pass, and you know they've been paid from work. You think, "Well, it's only $20." Six months later, they're posting on Facebook about skiing. You call them, asking about their trip and you mention the $20 they owe you. The next time you see them, they pay you back. The profound question is, "When will you ever lend *that* friend $20 again?" The answer is never; trust is broken.

The expectation is that your dog's big, strong, omnipotent, omniscient human surrogate parent **must** know whenever they're scared. As dog parents, it's imperative to demonstrate protection from psychological and physical threats to address and prevent dysfunctions beyond "innate" and "fear," which are predicated on the many defining structures of fear. These ultimately are coincident structures.

You're having a bad day at work. For no apparent reason, your best friend calls to check in on how you're doing. You're surprised and happy. You think, "You somehow knew I was having a bad day! This is why we're best friends!" In reality, we'll have 300 bad days in a year, yet no one calls on those other days.

Here's another example: you usually have a great day at work, but one day, you have a "very, very bad workday." You need to talk to someone you trust. You won't call the friend who tells you your job sucks, your boss doesn't appreciate you, and that you should quit. Instead, you call the person who helps you feel better–the person who talks you out of quitting. That's an intuitively predicated salient decision despite your emotional upset. You seek help, empathy, protection, and defense. You need nurture despite your nature, to seek a manner of escape, also known as "flight, then fight" emotionally.

It's a highly scathing indictment of academia's proliferation of failed theories, ultimately proving that expert academia is inept. Humans are among the largest, most glaringly apex specie. The practice of dominance or leadership is a result of inexperience. Dominance is the insecurity of the dog expert, reflecting a lifelong miscomprehension that overlooks the blatantly disproportionate differences. It furthers naivety of transactive behavior, such as "leader."

Using "fear" indicates miring in the permafrost of "innate," unable to trust their intuition beyond their own fears, and to disaggregate and destructure dysfunctions intelligently. Generalizations of behavior betray science's obligation to learn the granular–slivers of the granules. The threads and wisps of traits of sentient psychology <u>always</u> offer accurate, destructure-able reasons for dysfunction. The inept rely on *behavioral euthanasia*.

Like a child at a birthday party sitting alone, the inference is conveyed through self-marginalization and overt disparity. The elicitation of human patterning within empathetic structuring is not pareidolia or anthropomorphism but rather species-congruence, where identifiable emotives psychosomatically manifest in nuanced behaviors. It's the child hearing your tone within familial-words: viscerally, through intonation, rhythm, cadence, inflection, etc. All familial-species empathetically and introvertively process everything.

It has always been parency–a product of physical and psychological, structurally intradependency. Human fragility and insecurity default to a superficial transactive declaration of "leadership" being effective. This taciturn academic abuse by humans, being the apex dominion, instills performative fear in dogs. Imagine living with someone who will ultimately make the final decisions on everything, often without consulting you. Remember how much you disliked adults "always telling you what to do?" Lacking the experience to recognize nonverbal communication or comprehend the ills of subjugation teaches dogs to <u>confirm</u> you <u>**aren't**</u> understanding their blatant nonverbal cues; this forces dogs to behave in the only way they can–defensively and physically–resulting in negative psychological interactions.

Dogs behave negatively with their mouths, while humans recoil, concerned about being bitten. Communication becomes superficial, and the relationship devolves into transactional interactions. Your dog learns you don't comprehend their emotional expressions or overall sense of self. Therefore, dysfunctions manifest gradually, then with greater concentration. This ironic anthropomorphic decry by academics with hypocritical opines.

Your dog succumbs to their default emotive structures of rage and joy due to a lack of idiomatic, contextual self-actualization caused by experts being physically afraid, miscomprehending behavior as generic.

"Fear" transcends species, deeply rooted in primal emotional responses to survival. The label stagnates intuition. Behavior is extremely hyper-detailed, constructed in both functional and dysfunctional structures. Familial-species, such as dogs and humans, experience fear with a profound visceral comprehension. Entirely introverted and introspective, dogs and animals don't need complex, premeditative, fantastical ideation as do humans, whose conduct is governed by materialist superficiality; hence, guile, cajolery, and similar deliberate manipulations are attainments sought for self-aggrandizement.

Fear isn't the wholesale label. Fear comprises aggregates from the individual's numerous historical and present circumstances, contextualized into idiomatic relevance for egoistic structure, processing comparatives for historical reference. This emotion is not the "sum of our parts" but the constant conflation of all circumstances, both separately and together, for reciprocal processing. This isn't direct competition within the functional core of consciousness-logic processes but a contemporaneous concomitant of logic and illogic. Logic competes with the illogic of emotive structures as an attempt to figure out what's happening, why we feel as we do, and what options to self-soothe and self-actualize–nurture and nature.

Depart from the bane of academia's historically incestuous lineal learnings, which have relied on uniformly failed predecessors accoladed despite their lack of even moderate success. Fear is academia's band-aid descriptor, being unable to fathom deeper wounds, whilst attempting to tamp down fantastical ideation psychosomatically manifesting in "training sessions" while unaware of its centrality to egocentric cognizance. Consider the psychological antonym of fear as the wholesale structure of love. It's *not* indifference or hate; those are merely banal attachments. Indifference is neutrally implied. Emotive motivation predicates objectification and complex, evolved empathy.

Are Dogs Naturally Attached to Humans?

Let's examine the basic three emotional dependency structures: inter-, co-, and intra-dependency.

Domesticated dependency is human surrogate parenting. Dependency arises from a profound sense of safety and trust provided to each other. Connection is nurtured through support, care, and emotional interaction between them. There can't be friendship, companionship, or reliance on others without emotive dependency—the quantification of consciousness due to sophisticated emotive construction. Dependency is the epitome of reciprocating emotionally congruent loyalty. We expect those with whom we share a contiguous positive emotional attachment to be there for us when we need them.

Codependency can be both healthy and unhealthy. Your best friend or a coworker you love working with...similar <u>healthy</u> codependency exists between best friends. The relationship may be lopsided, but emotionally, there is cogent, isomorphic maturation for both parties. Both evolve their objectification and empathetic structure.

Intradependency: evolutionally predicated, yet intrinsically inter-relational, inter-habitative, familial structure by default. It's the first development of "dependency" as the whole psychological structure. Intradependency is imperatively foundational for sophisticated familial-species such as dogs' and humans' evolving sense of self and development of empathy via objectification. Intradependency occurs upon birth and aging onward. There exists obligatory intradependency between two such individuals. Emotions, experienced individually, create parallel emotive structures in each other. Intradependency begets codependency, which is construable, either healthy or unhealthy, relative to the relationship's fitness. Two people in love describe their relationship as soulmates. That is intradependency. Remember classmates who were absolute best friends and hung out together all the time; then, one of them moved away, leaving the other sad and lonely, grieving their loss.

Between infant and parent is entirely intradependent. Reliance on food, mobility, comfort, and safety—as well as emotional, psychological, and physical protection—is implicit in parency. The intradependency that locally evolves in the child is literally encouraging the development of self-objectification and empathetic structure. From there, codependency evolves into greater independence. Intradependency exists fulsomely between child and parent.

Disrupting this natural bond, dogs become narrowly ego-selfish and introverted by outwardly behaving negatively. Dogs and humans will develop a sense of insecurity and a need to protect themselves because they perceive a lack of familial protection, which they expect from their larger, stronger human surrogate parent. Protecting oneself is consequential and sequential to "flight, **then** fight."

Your role as human surrogate parents is to nurture healthy dependencies.

Dogs comprehend contrived domestication, and these attachments are clearly rooted in humans' seemingly free provision of trust, care, and mutual affection to dogs. Our empathy is cognizable to our dogs. Here's an analogy: ever watch a foreign-language film without subtitles? Or watch two people in love sitting at a table? You intuitively process the body language from your historical-comparative conflated of similar circumstances, aligned contexts, and emotive representations. Your human "predator" is no different than your dog's "predator" in identifying, with reasonable accuracy, the physical behaviors and facial expressions, and level of animation of their focus or target. Just as a predator can recognize juvenile or immature physical behavior–or "smell fear."

It's essential to recognize that every dog is uniquely individual. The goal should be to help your dog develop a healthy level of self-esteem, self-worth, and self-confidence while maintaining your dog's ego and introspection. Proving to your dog that you will protect them in a familial context helps build a healthy, loving, and trusting bond.

Idiomatic Contextualization

Whether domesticated or wild, dogs need to develop structural egoselfishness–the understanding of their place, regardless of whether within or outside the human-specie world. Idiomatic contextualization is crucial for dogs, humans, and other moderate-to-sophisticated familial-species–emotional personal relevance built through the aggregative conflation of historical comparisons.

The circumstances we are involved in, whether we are physically present or merely told about by another party, default to contextualizing relevance in terms of emotional value for you. How you perceive the world and consciousnessly process it, constantly aggregating circumstances for historical reference, is compartmentalized based on your emotional and logical perspectives about it. Although your sense of self and perception are relevant only to you, they are structured in an atypical way and yet replicated individually across each familial-specie in a homogeneous, corresponding dilution scale. Objectification is emotionally central to you, the idiomatic perceiver. What's "experienced" is constructed as a circumstance, personally relevant. An emotive structure is biologically contextualized within the physical brain's consciousness structure. Evolutionarily, fantastically ideative construction creates self-directing salience, transcribing what is happening, witnessed, or heard, customized to each individual's consciousness and perception. It causes perspective to evolve into personality-driven autonomic.

It teaches your "self" how to process what's being experienced. Your "self" learns how it feels emotively within/against your logical processing. Consciousness creates a mnemonic context along with prior similarities, including remotely similar and contrasting memories, as well as contextually similar emotives. Emotionally prioritized context can preempt reasoning and logic processing due to evolution physiologically compartmentalizing circumstances (egocentrically). Happening simultaneously are plurality relevances comparing current circumstances. Stored contextualized, interpreted upon the introspective ability to understand. This requires the emotives to find a foundation by funneling into the memory-specificity of context. Hence, emotions are relevant to the individual, creating idiomatic contextualization–both defaulting to compartmentalization of emotive constructs and compartmentalization through psychological-biological deliberateness.

Your Dog Wants You to Protect Them

The opine that "your dog is protecting you" is erroneous. It's arrogance as if the human-specie is automatically evolutionally more valuable than other species relative to familial cohabitation. Dogs are not inherently obedient to you nor do they protect you due to their nature. Propagated by the arrogant declaration: "Humans domesticated dogs." A misconstrual. "Dogs are protective standing by you" is an anthropomorphistic conjecture. Reiterating: the familial structure of dogs and humans is the same, characterized by parenthood and protection from humans to children and dogs. Parents empirically prove they're always protecting.

Using the bathroom, your dog follows or sits by the door. Your dog knows where their home's ingress and egress is. Logically, your dog would be guarding those doors. Being in the bathroom betrays cogency; an intruder would need to enter the home first, nor does your dog know what you're doing on the toilet. Your toilet functions similarly to sitting in a chair in the kitchen while working on your laptop. Your dog doesn't care when you go to the bathroom since your dog goes to the bathroom in public. There's zero sense to "fight" danger on one's doorstep. You don't draw danger home. In war, enemies are drawn away from each other, pushing back to the enemy's own doorstep. We observe a similar behavior in the actions of wild animals with their babies when confronted by a predator. Animal parents draw predators away from their young. It's antithetical of logic of war and nature.

Human analogy: you're walking with your stronger, bigger partner. Sketchy people walk toward you; your partner will protectively move closer and switch sides with you so they are nearest to the potential threat, putting you to safety furthest away.

Having abandoned our intuitive appreciation of psychosomatic manifestation, losing our attunement to these cues, and erroneously decrying them as anthropomorphism, we can absolutely decipher and quantify behaviors and relative to the human-specie.

"Triggers" and "Threshold"

"Fear-based aggression" is circumstantial. Stimuli evoke emotive defaulting due to unfamiliarity–an analogy is dating someone who doesn't like holding hands in public. As much as you try, they won't. As your relationship matures, their trust and love strengthen...six months later, they're holding your hand in public. You say nothing because you don't want to emotionally embarrass them, or they might stop holding hands. Familiarity evolves introvertive and ego-selfish health.

Dogs that *appear* not to like affection may walk away. Others may turn and bite you due to unfamiliarity with complex, foreign emotions that conflict introvertively. Dogs subjected to physical abuse are consternated, contextualizing within their sense of safety. Their natural physical competency, relative to flinch response and hypersensitivity, is due to an inherent proclivity to attempt cogent processing.

"Triggers"–be they loud noises, unfamiliar surroundings, or specific gestures–unlock understanding of behavior, which works at the speed of evolved aggregation and causal instinct development. Dogs possess unique personalities, and it is important to recognize that these are not mere "thresholds" but constructs of rudimentary logic and emotive processing structures. Academics must rescind conceit so as to rehabilitate dysfunctional dogs out of a state of distress.

Positive Association Irretrievably Damaged Academia

Positive association has its genesis attributed to Ivan Pavlov but was further misconstrued by B.F. Skinner. Ian Dunbar's inexperience leads him to opine that dysfunctional dogs not complying with food, medication, or other stimuli have no hope of rehabilitation and should be killed. Ian routinely refers to dogs as "it." His dogma–*behavioral euthanasia*–has been parroted by "aggression experts" such as James Crosby, Melanie Uhde, Erin Hecht, Claudia Richter, Rebecca Ledger, Stanley Coren, Michael Shikashio, Michael Ellis, and other North American leading experts. All declined affluent Southampton Animal Shelter's requests to rehabilitate Walter. A consensus claimed that Walter couldn't be rehabilitated or medicated sufficiently, even with far greater dosages than David. Their ineptitude confluent their human fear and inexperience while masquerading professional malpractice, needlessly killing dysfunctional dogs. *Positive association* is an explicit professional failure, miscomprehending the world's most prolific cross-species domesticate and inanely thinking of praise and reward as intrinsic counter to dysfunction.

The canine species fight to the death over food, as Charles Darwin observed. Giving a dysfunctional dog food literally elicits and enables predator instinct. It's giving an angry child having a temper tantrum a new toy. It's giving a drug addict more drugs. Nowhere in the canine species is food used as a communication device, reward fiat, or a performative compliance mechanism. You won't see one wolf bringing a piece of carrion to another wolf for a "good job."

Notwithstanding the complex emotive structure obligating empatheticism–especially in highly contextualized circumstances such as fighting–we don't see two gorillas about to attack each other, with a third gorilla trying to prevent the fight by giving both of them bananas.

Logic debunks the concept of consciousness, demarcating complex dysfunctions as "human-exclusive."

Say it's summer, and you're a passenger in a car. Your driver is an excellent professional. You drive through an intersection with a fresh green light when someone runs their red light and t-bones your side of the car. You're severely injured and hospitalized for months. You have to relearn how to walk and feed yourself with a spoon. Cognitively, you're okay.

After discharge, you have to take a car to get home. The driver is slow and cautious–stopping at every stop sign and watching every intersection. They drive exactly as you ask them. As you get closer to home, you realize you're approaching the same intersection where the accident happened. You're very anxious. You become terrified. Your breathing quickens. Entering the intersection, you feel trauma begin to overwhelm you; you struggle to control a panic attack while hyperventilating. Then the driver turns to you and gives you an ice cream cone. Trauma reflects a seemingly uncontrollable extreme of psychological and emotional upset which operates within a very narrow band. Just as with Mingki's emotions held within a cement pipe. Yet, we experience lesser degrees of narrow emotive processing such as having an argument with a friend. When the argument escalates into full-blown yelling as you remain steadfast yet belligerent in your debate position, imagine your friend suddenly handing you your most favorite chocolate bar from your childhood. Their action may cause you to shift emotionally higher, become even more upset or completely exasperated. You might even take the chocolate bar (materialist-predation) yet continue angrily. Rather than the chocolate bar ameliorating or pacifying, you are inconsolable in your anger. This tendril downstreams with the construction of trauma structures.

Breaking the Cycle of Academic and Professional Fear of Dangerous Dogs

When ten PhD behavioral scientists study a very dysfunctional dog, they try various methods. When all ten fail, they kill the dog. The ten scientists live, having learned nothing other than anecdotally deficient attributions of *behavioral euthanasia*. Ten scientists continue–dog after dog is killed. Scientists don't attain elicitation of their higher-instinct functioning to assimilate behavior correctly. There's no evolutionally-predicated survival elicited. No human instinct is elicited for comprehension in evolutional construction. No primal fear inter alia circumstance. No eliciting anthropomorphic intuition. No evolutional incentive to stay alive therefore no greater function of consciousness is engaged. To guide our dogs through the maze of psychological dysfunctions beyond "fear," sophisticated empathy must be our guiding light. We *must* remember that dog and animal behavior is psychologically similar to humans relative to biological sophistication.

A safe-harbor sanctuary through healthy parenting offers correlatory understanding as we cohabitatively evolve our structure of empathy. Emotive isomorphism isn't pertinent due to a lack of evolutional relevance. We can navigate *their* fears together, rebuild trust in their world again, and modernize academia from anthropomorphically victimizing dysfunctional dogs with death. Through compassionate interactions, patience, guidance, and a commitment to dogs' emotional well-being, we can lead any dysfunctional dog towards full rehabilitation–true healing of your dog's Soul.

Part 5
Historical Perspective and Conceptual Issues of Dog's Behavior

CHAPTER 10

Behavioral Ecological Aspects

The Role Dogs Play in Ecological Balance

The introduction of dogs into *our* world wasn't a remarkable opportunity of fate in the grand narrative of evolution–it was a coincidence. Evolution's specificity and success for any species premises on population: the volume-random substantiation by mathematical frequency of key anomalies populating within the specie's iterations. Commonalities mathematically funneled as traits, becoming standard features. The emergence of dogs on our planet is a part of random evolution, just like the emergence of humans. The possession of consciousness, ergo, the emotive ego, exhibits selfish psychology, which is isomorphic in consciousness and the empathetic structure of direct descendants.

The emotional commonality is the flagrance of emotional isomorphic flexibility, and that is true accommodation, as is the need for evolutionary construction. Evolution favors traits that are most conducive and efficient, allowing them to advance despite stochastic fluctuations, such as common trait sequences that are popularized through propagation. It's comprehensible that evolution's economy is a resource- and mathematically-conservative, and therefore cannot sustain two wholly different consciousnesses, globally intermingled. Clearly divergent yet fundamentally based on the exact first-cell engineering schematics. Intuitive comprehension via empathetic objectification in recognition of the emotional richness of others and other species.

Early humans were not objectively derisive of other species due to the understanding that other species would likely possess similar self-awareness. "Therefore, I am." Despite the human arrogant perspective that all other species are lesser, the practices and beliefs of early humans comprehended their environment as cooperative and appreciative. Early humans didn't speak verbally; hence, body language, considered a universal form of communication by all species, is cognitively important.

The coincidental ecological exposure between our two species allowed humans to develop the capacity to feel emotions publicly towards other species, further extrapolating introverted objectification with emotional and social context established via familial idiomatic contexting. Before humans cohabitated knowingly, albeit accidentally, and created the first offspring, there needed to be an empathy sophisticated enough to develop between the two human-specie genders, from infatuation to emotional, idiomatic, and familial importance. This objectification extends beyond the introvertive motivation of self-satisfaction attainment (e.g., egocentric) by creating a cogent awareness of *me* and *others*, leading to a profound sense of self through the appreciation of other humans and other species, achieved through observation and direct witness. The introspection of objectification led to the psychological construction of an empathetic structure.

This newfound growing visceral empathy played a pivotal, evolutionary role in shaping human societies' default to broader, emotive generosity. Self-awareness is objectified, thus promoting the development of preferred societal dependency. Ironically, visceral empathy didn't extend from humans to other species, no matter how intimately other familial-species were integrated into our evolving domestication through societal association and ecological adherence to common, shared perspectives, such as "live and let live." Dogs have been immensely loyal to humans throughout millennia. The human-specie missed the consciousness of dogs due to the decrees of the church and chronic academic arrogance. Instead, finding *usefulness* in animals as performative assets is ultimately utilitarian. This materialist possessiveness is a human-specie's mistake; materialist predation is evolutionarily ingrained in every trait and nuance of the human-specie while denigrating itself toward self-extinction.

Sadly, dogs remain political utilities despite "30,000 years" of pursuing prey together, proving their fierce loyalty, even at the cost of their own lives. Politicians continue to deem dogs as property, and the courts, without mature cognizance, fail to recognize their sophisticated sentience. This is the <u>sole</u> fault of academia.

Dogs are killed with delusional euphemisms such as "destroyed" and "put down," or under crass prevarications like "put to sleep" and "behavioral euthanasia," which betrays unwavering loyalty to have dysfunctional dog killing be described as crassly incidental. Dogs were eaten by the Chinese, Koreans, Vietnamese, Africans, and other peasant populations.

The human specie's ingratitude is demonstrated by all police departments, which deliberately refuse to protect their police dogs with K9 bulletproof vests. While courts are played by craven police lawyers claiming, with discordancy, that police dogs be afforded the same legislative protection as human police, yet negligently not protected similarly. Police and prosecutors push for long imprisonments that, in many cases, were **preventable** police-dog deaths. The police's utility of dogs is irrefutable proof that police dogs are *wink-wink* forced into *death jobs*. The police handler disingenuously cares for police dogs, evidenced by their apathy towards equal protection. By perverting dogs' gentle, intradependent familial predispositions into attack roles, the police knowingly contribute to the vicious reputation of the specie, leaving each police dog as a life of lesser value–waiting for criminals to strike.

Most law enforcement/military K9 units do **NOT** purchase life-saving "$1,400 vests.[38]

Police prove police dogs are expendable property. Dogs have no idea they are running into danger of suffering catastrophic injury. Nor do they understand that their deaths could be violent. In America and Canada, more than 60,000 police and military dogs are killed once *retired,* as their adoptability is extremely limited–an act of staggering human reprehensibility.[39] Hundreds of dogs die during police-dog training programs due to heat or exhaustion. Some police dogs are even hung by their *handler* on their leash. "Wink wink." Were you to commit such psychological and physical acts, you would be arrested for criminal animal cruelty.

Dogs afford humans the grandeur of sophisticated empathy. Human control over the life of each and every dog, from pre-civilization and pre-agrarian human barbarity to the present-day dominion of all animals. This conceit provided humanity's materialist evolution–a tacit callousness that we wield heavily and wantonly. Their manageable size made it possible for early humans to establish bonds, as we confidently know we hold death over all dogs. Our confidences are facades. It's more than a mere suggestion; without dogs, our society would be more predatory unto itself and emotively

---

[38] Project Paws Alive, "K9 Vests Bullet Stab," accessed September 16, 2025, https://ppak9.org/k9-vests-bullet-stab/.

[39] Paws of Honor, "Law Enforcement Officers and Police Dogs Deserve Our Support," accessed September 16, 2025, https://pawsofhonor.org/law-enforcement-officers-and-police-dogs-deserve-our-support/

truncated. Dogs play a crucial role in inspiring and fostering a greater complexity of empathy and cooperation through shared cohabitation and familial dependency. The consciousness of dogs has remained consistent in qualifying their domestic companionship as an extension of our emotional connection and sense of empathy; it continues to evolve.

What Dogs Need in Their Environment

"Dogs need jobs" is a miscomprehension. Behavior isn't a preoccupation. At its root, consciousness relies on rudimentary logic and emotive processing structures. The latent guilt humans superficially experience in their misplaced emotional processing is a manifestation of human inadequacy, not dogs being *bored*.

The current marketing of *smart cognitive dog toys*, such as snuffle mats and puzzle toys, often fails to deliver the cognitive benefits promised. Dogs usually smell their environment. Smelling provides context for the environment and the spatial process of time. The commercial dog market falls prey to the miscomprehensions of inept dog behaviorists. The era of *cognitive toys* is anthropomorphic, transactive-performative, and simpleton logic-predicated. There's no idiomatic relevance. Contextualization is lineal. Addressing emotional comprehension relative to the threshold is where the overall maturation of the individual must sustain interest beyond humanistic anecdotes. Currently, there are no cogency toys. Cogency elicits broader emotive development for complex introspective processing, allowing time to process idiomatically.

Cognitive toys are performative and transactive, providing limited opportunities for emotional development–no room for emotional elaboration. There is no opportunity for a leisurely experience nor a clearer, stronger construction or development. Such experiences are delayed due to processive *duress*.

Wolves seek food and a safe, manageable region to domestically call home–without schedules or task-based transactions. If an area established by a wolf family (or lion family pride) were suddenly to appear comfortable, with indestructible beds housed within a secure area sheltered from the elements and food *magically* appearing daily (whether randomly or on a fixed schedule), they would use their cogence to adjust their predation strategies accordingly and develop a sport of predation to fine-hone continuously during life, and benefiting their progeny. Over generations, this will lead to greater familial stabilization within the species while maintaining significant competitive predation skills. This demonstrates the evolvement of emotive consciousness construct. Wolves are not naively contending, though caution must be exercised to not label as "habituating" to contrived domestication. Wild bears, hyenas are apt the same. Emotive isomorphism.[40]

As discussed in my commentary, "Why The Wolf Sadistically Mutilated Livestock[41]," these behaviors highlight the complexities of domestication and its beneficial influence on "wild" familial-species' visceral cogency, at scale.

While rich countries kill dogs wantonly, privately-funded rescue organizations in second and third-world countries house tens of thousands of dogs. Groups of hundreds eagerly run to the food cart, waiting for breakfast. The intrinsic urgency of hunger is self-placated individually by the thought that food is imminently guaranteed: homogeneity despite born predation.

Dogs comprehend with emotional similarity, at corresponding dilutive scale. Dogs aren't looking for constant excitement. Dogs are burst predators, not endurance predators. Dogs thrive when they feel safe and protected. Our role as human caregivers is to provide this sense of familial security.

What Is the Behavioral Adaptation of a Dog?

Behavioral adaptation in dogs is a cautionary tale for academia, following the miscomprehensions of Skinner et al, while ignorantly anthropomorphizing conjectures and literally ascribing behavior as a Boolean. Behavioral adaptation is causal compliance. It's the anthropomorphization of bartering. It's quid pro quo cajoling. It omits introspective cogency.

Dogs and children aren't born with a comprehensive understanding to process their emotions, especially their egos. Dogs and children can't self-actualize or self-soothe complex emotive structures without prior familiarity. There's no adaptation without learning idiomatic emotive contextualization.

---

40 Saveafox, "Education on the misconceptions of wild Black bears," *YouTube*, posted July 27, 2024, https://www.youtube.com/watch?v=vDkYbaLgnQ0.

41 Arf Arf Bark Bark Rescue & Rehab, "Why The Wolf Sadistically Mutilated Livestock - Sept 9, 2022, *YouTube*, posted September 9, 2022, https://www.youtube.com/watch?v=f2-jn7SIKDY.

All familial-species need help in understanding and contextualizing their complex emotions in relation to their circumstances. Truthful adaptation hinges on your ability to help dogs understand the emotions they experience and how to respond appropriately.

Behavioral and Environmental Enrichment

Classical behavioral and environmental enrichment is archaic. What holds true is teaching dogs to psychologically grasp the intricate web of their emotions and contextualize them within their functional sentience. Dogs learn about their body and have dimensional awareness and objectification. Surroundings are equally acknowledged in the context of circumstantial processing.

It's amusing to read about researchers placing dogs on mats with toys tied to them to see if they will recognize that standing on the mat is consequential. Dogs don't comprehend physics in the same human-like manner. It fails to develop their selfishness by teaching how to contextualize relevance to their circumstances idiomatically. Cogency over cognitive, every time.

Social Behavior: Interaction with the Human-Specie

Affection and Trust

Dogs seek affection from their human surrogate parents in various ways. It's extremely crucial to consistently sustain healthy intradependency and healthy codependency. Keys to establishing beautiful familial relationships are remembering that your dog's response time is faster than half of one-tenth of a second, which means cogency is equally efficient and simple. Hypersensitivity and flinch-response are extremely superior. Dogs feel vibrations from thunder, heavy truck traffic, and fireworks due to the omnidirectional movement of sound. Dogs don't comprehend the physics of sound. Dogs can't ascertain the source, causing some concern. Here's an analogy: when you're home alone and hear scary noises, you will look for the source, yet you're terrified in case someone has broken into your home.

I keep my hands physically still and predictable—no patting, petting, rubbing, or vigorous movements. Movements create distractions, just as *shaking knees* shows nervousness. Stillness. Motionless. Even a finger-tremor causes distraction. It doesn't provide calm familial protection if your hand moves even slightly. Stillness builds the foundation for your dog to learn and trust that you're parentally protective and aware of the "unknown." Reliable calmness every time they need parental acknowledgment and protection. Another analogy: a child sleeping in their bedroom becomes very afraid when they hear thunder and see lightning. It runs to its parents' room for protection, and secondarily, for comfort. If the parent comforts it by holding it in a hug but starts patting its back or quickly rubbing their hand up and down its back, the child might say, "Stop moving your hand and just hold me." It knows it's being distracted instead of feeling safe and protected by its parent. Your dog understands the importance of feeling protected and safe, which is conveyed through your calmness. Another helpful analogy is: as a child, when you got in big trouble and had to tell your parents, you sought out the parent who was calmer and more understanding. You inherently know they would protect you from the angrier parent.

You've probably heard: "Don't hug your dog" or "Dogs don't like to be hugged." This is counterintuitive to familial-species. It stems from humanly alpha-dominant leader dogma, lacking real-life experience, and belies a fear of being attacked.

Swallowing is often misinterpreted as stress. It is a highly complex, emotive process that physiologically manifests in your dog's jaw and head, which your dog physically feels–consciousnessly controlling their complex foreign emotives by swallowing. It's your dog counting to ten when experiencing foreign emotional complexity instead of negatively interacting. Swallowing represents the core intimate structure of familial-emotional trust, residing in constructional aspects. It's not entirely accurate to claim that swallowing is stressful.

"Bunny the Talking Dog" Retarding Behaviorism

In June 2020, I directly criticized Bunny's[42] mom, Alexis Devine, on her TikTok for leading behaviorism astray. She defended herself, then deleted most of my comments and blocked me. Two hours later, I was notified she'd replied. I surmise she googled me. I was absolutely aghast to learn she had corralled equally inept behaviorists into her delusion.

---

42 https://en.wikipedia.org/wiki/Bunny_(dog)

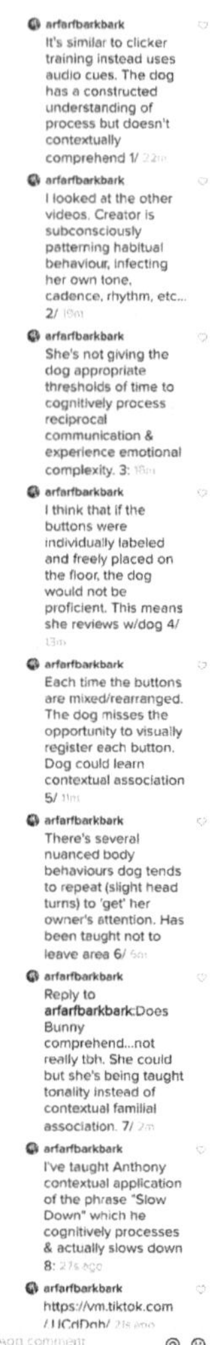

I demonstrate context association and cogency training with Anthony. The first video shows teaching Anthony the context of the phrase "slow down", helping him understand situational cues and appropriate responses as does a child.[43] The second video illustrates teaching Anthony the objectification of the phrase "can of tuna" in just twenty minutes, highlighting rapid comprehension of verbal cues and associative learning.[44]

---

43 @arfarfbarkbark, TikTok video, "Teaching Anthony the Context of 'Slow Down'," https://www.tiktok.com/@arfarfbarkbark/video/6829875571409931526.

44 @arfarfbarkbark, TikTok video, "Teaching Anthony the Objectification of 'Can of Tuna' in 20 Minutes," https://www.tiktok.com/@arfarfbarkbark/video/6852848107659529477.

Alexis isn't the first to convince herself; she's teaching dogs to "speak" via talking buttons playing recorded words by her. Previously, a speech pathologist brought forth similar miscomprehension: she taught her dog Stella to "speak."[45]

I am extremely direct in my criticism. Alexis subtly cues Bunny in her highly edited videos. I cautioned Alexis that she would cause Bunny to become neurotic. Her videos were essentially a David Letterman *Stupid Pet Tricks* segment. No more.

It turns out that inept behaviorists, linguists, and others clamored to "study" Bunny. The inept led by the charlatan. While writing this book, I checked online to see what had been happening. I sadly laughed reading about Bunny's developed dysfunctions and that she is now needlessly medicated for psychosis.[46] I note that Alexis now has dog training accreditation, which appears intended to give herself validation and confidence despite her intrinsic awareness that her work is disingenuous.

Talking Buttons Debunked

1. *Talking buttons* pre-recorded with a human (Alexis') voice eliminates independent correlation (introvertive/self-objectification/egocentrism). They remove the idiomatic requirement for self-comprehension. Without a uniquely specific *voice*, connection is not egotistical but co- and intra-dependent, preventing introvertive construction. Biological communication, regardless, exhibits significant unique frequency modulations individually. Point of disenfranchisement: every time you use text-to-speech for *needed* things like food, affection, going out, going to play, or sleep—was it the voice of your dad? There is no translative idiomatism. It's not comprehensive structurally and requires neutrality for self-ego comprehension.
2. Hence, Bunny's years involved **should** show an increase in complexity, measurable by idiomatic expressions. But Bunny's medicated for neuroticism. Bunny's cognitive degradation is due to her emotive immaturation (neologism) because Alexis sustained contrived

[45] CNN, "A speech pathologist taught her dog Stella to 'speak,'" *YouTube,* posted November 9, 2019, https://www.youtube.com/watch?v=bJCxrc7Ns_g.

[46] *Daily Mail*, "TikTok Star Pup Asking for Anti-Depression Medication," Femail, November 17, 2022, https://www.dailymail.co.uk/femail/article-11622989/TikTok-star-pup-asking-anti-depression-medication.html

intradependency and imposed very low self-esteem, albeit Bunny's dysfunctions don't require psychopharmaceuticals.

3. *Talking buttons* have different colors. Alexis blithely changes words, colors, physical order, and shape, thinking she's constantly stimulating Bunny's syntax. Essentially, it removes Bunny's cogency and presumption structure, causing Bunny to be so comfortable with Alexis' proxy articulation. Bunny makes constructional syntax errors using the talking buttons, which connotes Bunny's self-awareness relative to the presumed reliability of *talking buttons*. Imagine that every time you drove to work, the city would change the traffic lights and appearance, alter roads, and change street names. Colors must be all the same or within a gradient.
4. Talking buttons are rudimentary *cognitive*. The approach fails the aggregative conflating structure of learning. Imagine your daily drive through the city, where the roads set ever-changing detours. The button's shape and order must NOT keep changing. Analogy: It would be like waking up to find your keyboard rearranged overnight–what was once "QWERTY" is now scrambled nonsense.
5. In Alexis' highly curated videos, Bunny can't create sentences or demonstrate semantic and idiomatic cogency. It's naive to postulate that dogs articulating via *talking buttons* is congruent with a six-year-old child whose entire life, immersed in English from kindergarten through second grade, is unable to grammatically or idiomatically structure language sentences proficiently, but Bunny and other talking-button dogs can. An entirely different specie, with no prior familiarity of expressively rigid formal articulable ability, can then functionally converse in another specie's (human) language. When Bunny wants to "talk" outside or in other contexts, it is simply a compromise of logic.

Truthfully, Bunny is Clever Hans.[47] The desperation to ascribe anthropomorphic competency to Bunny profoundly damages behaviorism. It's Clever Hans-Dunning-Kruger behaviorism. Their contention implies cogency for alien complex novelty existing beyond functional anomaly, ergo, within the canine specie (perhaps only in "domesticated" ones?). Truly specious.

---

[47] https://en.wikipedia.org/wiki/Clever_Hans

Cognitive Decline in Dogs

Physical health issues can contribute to cognitive decline in dogs due to a depressive influence. Deterioration of introspective objectivity and compromised egocentrism can lead to self-marginalization, such as self-exiling and feelings of being *unwanted* (abandonment structure).

Dogs who have experienced emotional trauma, neglect, or abuse develop cognitive-emotive issues. Stress, anxiety, and depression all impact your dog's cognitive abilities. Human analogy: you attend an event where you know everyone, and everyone is genuinely happy to see you...yet you feel a million miles away–not as a function of paranoia, but as an affectation of your sense of self-esteem.

It's a common misconception that dogs "operate on instinct and simple/learned behaviors." However, as I've observed and studied dogs extensively, it's clear to me that our opportunity to comprehend consciousness is being squandered. It's not cognition that you want to develop in your dog; it's cogency.

The Future of Canine Cogency

I'm committed to expanding the understanding and comprehension of canine cogency. My work challenges the conventional wisdom that dogs lack sophisticated consciousness. Cognition research is an unsophisticated approach. My theorem of consciousness and learning explain the cogent abilities of dogs in the context of evolution. Cognition is genericism. We must stop underestimating consciousness in familial-species as if evolution no longer functioned advent humanity. Dogs recognize problem-solving in their environment and rely on physics as understood physically.

Cogency Games

Teaching your dog, just like a child, the front, back, and which side their paws are–for example, "Nero's back left foot"–provides introspective comprehension and objectification of who they are as a three-dimensional individual: self-objectification. You provide your dog with *empirical* confirmation that you're aware they have different sides to them and comprise a physical individual. You provide dimensional comprehension relative to idiomatic objectification, sharing with your dog that you understand they have different body parts. Thus, providing self-esteem relative to self-image (introspective structure). This develops empathetic comprehension. Another cogency activity:

- Peanut Butter Plate, for left/right preference, is a cogent interaction. Take a dinner plate slightly larger than your dog's head. On exactly opposite sides of the plate, place two equal amounts of peanut butter (or another food your dog likes). Let your dog decide which side to start licking. Repeat this over several consecutive days. Track which side your dog chooses. This will indicate whether they prefer the left or right side. Your dog can visually see both dollops, yet will lick the side they prefer.

A Bittersweet Reflection

I share these insights acutely aware of the challenges ahead. My work may not gain the recognition it deserves until it's too late. It's a race against time to ensure that the knowledge I've accumulated is not lost to obscurity. I fear my books and ideas may remain undiscovered. I believe the world can significantly benefit from my empirical understanding. I remain hopeful that my work finds its way into the minds of future generations, who will build upon my theorem to advance human understanding of evolutionary consciousness. I hope that smarter people, judges, and politicians will advance my goal for dogs to be recognized as Functional Sentient Beings, afforded Limited Legal Rights. It's a daunting task, but one I believe is essential for the long-term well-being of the human-specie surviving for one million years.

My greatest fear isn't for myself. My publisher knows I've debated internally for years whether I should complete *The Soul of a Dog*. I'm not confident whether the human-specie deserves to be non-extinct. I hope that my work will serve as a source of guidance and inspiration for those who seek to improve the lives of dogs—and, more importantly, comprehend the evolutionary construction of consciousness before human self-extinction through materialist-predation.

CHAPTER 11

Understanding How Dogs Process Time, Pain, and Dependency (Intra/Co/Inter)

How Dogs Experience Time

Dogs, humans, and the majority of comparable familial-species experience time contextually. Time is psychologically relevant, though not necessarily idiomatic. Time isn't a tangible commodity considered relevant in any manner, except to humans, for embellishment. The measure of time is processed as an endurance of emotive measure. Individuals experience time through the phasing of their psychological process, occurring in emotive circumstances, as opposed to a linear progression.

For example, when you're doing something very fun and the activity ends, you might reflect, "I was having so much fun I didn't notice how quickly the time passed." Conversely, during a tedious lecture, you might think, "I'm sooo bored; this hour feels like an entire day of lecture." In both cases, time is compressed or expanded based on emotive endurance, making it psychologically taxing. Time is illogical without linearity. Humans demand egocentric valuation of time, asserting authority and control over abstract constructs.

Familial-species process time as a functionally emotive contexting of environment and circumstantial involvement. A dog that becomes angry when approached by a stranger will bark for as long as the individual remains emotionally upset. Some individuals bark briefly, while others continue for dozens of seconds or minutes, even after the stranger has left. This behavior refers to an individual's personality predilection, which is directly related to what the individual thinks and feels and is introspectively experienced. Whereas *human time* is cognitively ego-selfish, not egocentric.

Awareness of time exists across the full spectrum of feelings, including jealousy, rage, joy, and grief. For example, *boredom* might appear when your dog lies down, sometimes getting up to go to another room or the window to look outside. It's not rambunctiousness but rather a self-awareness of one's emotional status, spurred by introspective review.

When you tell your dog, "Let's go for a walk," they become excited, sustaining energy individually. If you're delayed by a phone call, your dog immediately notices the psychological impact of waiting. Emotions form foundation of impatience, which manifest as barking, pacing, lying down, or other nonverbal communication methods to encourage you to start the walk. These behaviors, aside from reflecting quantifiable measurements of consciousness, are fundamental manifestations influenced by the individual's perception of time, measured by the duration of the phone call—emotional fluctuation due to impatience. The complexity of how time is consciousnessly processed must include a logical combination. Not isolating as linear, which causes *time* to be unfathomable for destructure.

Time has never been linear, as humans demand selfishly. An individual specie's emotive structure comprises *who* they are. Dogs quantify their experience of time based on their introspection. The endurance of time is scaled to the emotional and psychological context rather than *length*. For dogs, *time* is experienced through patience, impatience, and other urgent and non-urgent emotional structures. The concept of measured time is that each circumstance experienced is a uniquely idiomatic circumstance weighted by its immediacy, emotional intensity, and comparative historic context; hence, the process of time is psychologically endured.

Humans' experience of time is lineal conceptually. We *see* memories but don't feel or endure their passage. Memories are literally timeless. Memory processing is fully attached to the emotive and psychological *measurement* of time. If we are confronted mentally with a traumatic dysfunction, we may or may not be able to endure its subject matter due to our psychological threshold. We endure the emotional context not as linear time but as illogic due to emotive connotation. Children experience time similarly to familial-species before being taught linear adherence through schedules and structured activities.

Time is not obligatory, whereas evolution is defaultively responsive. Cementing how dogs perceive time, there is an intrinsic emotional *intra-attachment* to the abstract measure of time, specifically compartmentalizing that circumstance within the structure of memory, creating a contextualized placement within consciousness predicated on an emotive construct. Yet, time is not logical for any specie other than human, whose transactiveness demarcates time. For domesticated dogs, time becomes a constraint due to humans defaulting to routine, which has convinced experts that "dogs need routine."

How is time abstractly experienced? Crudely, like an old-time slideshow projector– "Grandpa's Slide Film Projector."[48] Time is infinitely reducible. Each moment is experienced emotively in slivers of nuance. Dogs, animals, and children contextualize time much like each slide from an old-time projector: each slide contains a moment, and that moment is time-fluid despite being "captured in time." Each slide is from a different time. Still, in the projector's carousel, time is contextualized–albeit in a contrived linear way.

Time is infinitely length-reducible. Time is divisible and reducible within itself infinitely. The consciousness abstraction of each frame of time is, therefore, broken down into lesser and lesser measures of time. Each moment is broken into slivers of slivers of slivers–ad infinitum–which I wholly consider when destructuring dysfunctional behavior. Time functions from the function of neurotubules; Stuart Hameroff's theory of consciousness[49] skims lightly close to comprehending consciousness.

Dogs, like many sophisticated species, experience time in a fundamentally different manner than humans. There is a lack of complicated egoselfishness. There is no need to be "somewhere specifically." There is no planning–or rather, no fantastical, ideated speculation–such as setting your alarm clock to wake you at 6 a.m. However, if the alarm fails to go off or if you sleep through it, your scheduled plan is foiled.

No wild animals do things at exactly prescribed times. Human-specie plans span hours, days, even decades because they collectively *need* to measure their "start to finish" as an extension of *learning*. Just as I, as a child, planned for futuristic memory recall when I was a forty-something man. Our existence is questioned by our introvertive need to egocentrically understand why "I"

---

[48] FilterGrade, "Discovering my Grandpa's Old Slide Film Projector," *YouTube*, posted May 6, 2021, https://www.youtube.com/watch?v=4GtPU7elie4.

[49] Stuart Hameroff, "How Quantum Brain Biology Can Rescue Conscious Free Will," Frontiers in Integrative Neuroscience 6 (2012): Article 93, https://doi.org/10.3389/fnint.2012.00093.

exist and "How long do I have?" The human-specie bases its actions on the logic of time and, paradoxically, on the illogical obligation of time.

Memory works intra-attached with time. Time maintains the elasticity of the brain's consciousness structure development through callusing and biological contextualizing to *refresh* functionality. Memories are tangential stakes that adhere to the psychological context within the processing of consciousness, as what we do relates to what we remember. These can be considered bridges of how species, in general, process time.

Dogs don't ponder an abstract concept of time or consider its philosophical implications, for that is a predication of highly sophisticated materialism (egocentrism). Dogs don't attempt to control or manipulate time as humans do. Without sophisticated fantastical ideation or materialist affectation, there is no valued reason to quantify time.

How Dogs Process Pain

Pain is processed in contexts of redundancy and rhetoric. The key knowledge is the absence of demarcation or delineation between pleasure and pain. Pain is a gradient with pleasure.

When you're making your dog air-jog by rubbing or petting hypersensitive areas, the unfamiliar sensation is similar to being tickled. The movements are not reflexive per se. Air-jogging detracts from the actual enjoyment of physical intimacy. The psychological information published by organizations is often erroneous, such as the conjecture that equates yawning with the sensation of ticklishness, as seen in the article *Are Dogs Ticklish?*[50] Yawning is the cognitive dissipation of highly complex emotive structures and relates to circumstance.

Pain is a universally experienced phenomenon, but how do dogs perceive and process it? The human-specie notably articulates pain. Sophisticated species rely on similar biological mechanisms for processing physical pain within their consciousness' global structure–sophisticated species process pain through a combination of redundant and rhetorical contexting. Animals can't fulsome self-actualize what an injury feels like without psychological

[50] Elaine Waldorf Gewirtz, "Are Dogs Ticklish?" *American Kennel Club*, updated July 25, 2023, https://www.akc.org/expert-advice/lifestyle/are-dogs-ticklish/.

idiomatic context. The intensity of an injury doesn't typically have definitive comparative relevance. Pain is endured. Animals don't immediately recognize the cause of pain at initiation, even if the pain becomes enduring.

When your dog is running fast around a building, turns, but slips and hits the building, he gets up and runs almost immediately. Maybe he has a slight limp, but he seems to "shake it off." A hard enough impact clearly and responsively hurts your dog, causing limping. Acknowledgment of pain due to injury involves consciousnessly contextualizing the impact through introspective realization (problem-solving) of why and what happened, correlated with short-term, mid-term, and long-term memory to prevent recurrence of slipping, falling, and injury. It's not "learning from mistakes" but recognizing environment and causation, which is applied to similar circumstances.

An emotional connotation is created by idiomatically contextualizing the entire individualist experience of pain. Your dog will remember to adjust their approach next time and is unlikely to fall there again. At the same time, memory develops aggregatively. A trifecta creates optional thinking: "logic and illogic" introspectively creates a memory of what just happened. Pain is emotionally intradependent, not interrelational, entrenching short-term through long-term memory. Pain is not primarily an emotive catalyst but rather the psychological structure in which introspection occurs (though pain holds lesser cogency in the wild).

Pain is processed redundantly, such as when it is constant or repetitively occurring; it is psychologically cognizant. Pain is processed entirely ego-selfishly due to its exclusive first-party nature.

Pain processed rhetorically, for example, isn't a throbbing pain but rather a pain intensity of non-frequency/non-pattern and unexpected. Pain is immediately processed, and the expression of pain at onset is consciousnessly gauged by forced sustainment–observation of circumstance, environment, parties present, and cause of injury.

Pain tolerance is due to familiarity. If your dog is bitten by another dog, you inspect your dog's wound. Some will become ferociously upset when you touch their injury, while others will let their human parent clean their wound. There is a 100 percent intensity of pain in both scenarios. I've witnessed ignorant veterinarians callously poking and pulling at fresh stitches. Your dog is cogent with their complex physical pain, consciousnessly controlling one's desire for negative interaction relative to the intensity caused by pain. Your dog understands you're not the cause, which requires a sophisticated consciousness of pain coupled with environmental awareness.

Though your continued *touching* of the injury is 100 percent causing intense pain at the injury site, your dog controls the intra-default to rage. Naturally, there will be spikes of intense pain causing a greater upset, but it is objectively contexted amongst current pain levels–to which both contexts are processed rhetorically. Recurring as an enduring structure, knowingly accepting the cause of pain comprises self-objectification and furtherance of an empathetic structure.

Sophisticated consciousness learns to associate pain with tolerance and emotive reference, albeit pain contextualizes memory both mnemonically and viscerally. For example, you are walking in a pair of lace-up boots and you feel a tiny pebble in one boot. Aside from acute recognition of pain and discomfort, you'll continue walking to your destination instead of stopping to unlace and remove the pebble. Pain is tolerated redundantly by endurement.

Walking through your living room in the dark and stubbing your toe hard, you'll scream at the intensity of the pain, introverting it into manageability by compartmentalizing it into redundancy. This is not instinct, such as "suppressing pain to prevent predator awareness." You're not ignoring pain; you're enduring consistency using cogency to calm acute psychology.

Two months later, you stub the same toe again. You almost immediately recall the time prior, and your response is subdued due to circumstances, reconciliation, and personal responsibility. Your pain is processed as rhetoric despite its familiarity. Your first-time reaction is more animated than subsequent similar injuries due to historical familiarity.

The experience of pain manifests psychosomatically, always through behavior. Emotional control is what your injured dog cogently exercises. An injured individual doesn't keep crying because they're accustomed to the pain due to repetition. Note: every chemical reaction occurring biologically developed its construction through reconciling prior evolutionary designs, thus creating endorphins and similar responses, which occur coincidentally and responsively secondary such as to *pain* during the evolutionary period of pre-Darwinism. Not a subsequent result of.

Self-actualization in the context of pain processing. Individualistic emotional responses are deeply ingrained in a personality, predicated on the core default emotions. Dogs don't inherently comprehend unfamiliar physical sensations like pain or why it feels as such, without an idiomatic frame of reference to elicit introspective, ego-driven relevance. Pain is understood in relation to the environment and circumstances (such as during wartime).

Dogs comprehend pleasure–such as the pleasure derived from being calmly touched.

An example of redundant and rhetorical pain-processing despite significant intensity: a man cuts off arm.[51] The intensity of pain becomes tolerable through psychological redundancy.

Seemingly minor discomforts also illustrate this principle. For example, when your dog stares without blinking. The irritation of eyes drying is felt, and pain is processed rhetorically as sensation persists, eventually becoming compartmentalized and redundant. When carnivores chew **uncooked** raw bones, sharpness from broken bones is felt rhetorically *as a fact of life* when eating. Your dog's mouth is highly susceptible to texture, composition, and movement.

How Dogs Grieve

Dogs, with their profound capacity for emotional connections, experience grief when someone they deeply know passes away. When their presumption of regularity fails due to absence or death, it's a poignant function of sophisticated consciousness that reflects an evolved aptitude for forming deep, meaningful relationships predicated upon dogs' biological construction for emotional expression. How long had they known the decedent and the intensity of the relationship? We'll delve into the explanation of how dogs process grief. Understanding how other species mourn enhances the empathetic structure of the human-specie, contextualizes emotional richness on a larger scale, and, in turn, exemplifies consciousness as the functionally germane biology standard.

Grief behavior disaggregates into contextual structures, affecting short-term through long-term memory. At its core are the cogencies of *Permanence*

---

[51] https://en.wikipedia.org/wiki/Aron_Ralston

and *Permanence of Loss*–frames by which grief becomes idiomatically functional. Visitors, siblings, family, and family groups (including regularly interacting animals and humans) provide enduring emotional exposure for constructing comprehension of familial relationships and developing healthy codependency. Emotional connections endure, psychologically rooted in memory and introvertive contexting.

Sibling grief is similarly experienced when foster dogs come and go. Seemingly temporary or transient, the introduction of profound emotional change (*permanence*) in the familial construct is emotionally affective–the presumption of regularity of waking up every day to the same family. The circumstance of either beloved or foster leaving are no different other than semantic.

"Forever here" to "forever gone."

Dogs Don't Understand Death

Poignantly, your dog doesn't understand aging. Slowing down and physical ailments take time to become introspectively aware. Knowing one's death is possible, near, or imminent isn't learnable beyond gossamer. "Death being permanent and inevitable" is solely humanistic. Although your dog adjusts to their aging, this adjustment is a physically forced process. Throughout evolutional comprehension, introspectively understanding why they're not running as far or tiring quicker is translated physically. Your dog won't understand why they can't jump onto the couch as easily and painlessly. "Slowing down" and aging don't idiomatically contextualize due to complex abstraction. Knowing death is inevitable is a human comprehension. Dogs understand that something is physically "wrong," but not the abstract correlation.

As Nero began to Sunset, I would walk slower than him so he could still experience what he once did as a young dog freely[52], and to elicit latent visceral emotional and psychological memories as when Nero was young, running fast without pain of aging. Over the years, Nero had often heard people telling him to "slow down" on walks and laughing at his zoomie antics. By walking slowly together and "yelling" at Nero to slow down, Nero could remember those nostalgic, emotive contexts, continuing to build memory through idiomatic aggregation regardless of age. Latent memory

52 www.ArfArfBarkBark.com/NeroGreatDane/

for familial-species is similar to how humans experience fleeting memories or images, such as déjà vu.

Now let's discuss two fundamental global structures: *Permanence* and *Permanence of Loss*.

Permanence: Consciousness actively maintains mnemonic emotional knowledge of someone or something, functioning as a means of interaction; therefore, relevant and familiar emotives are sustained, contextualized, and cognizant of relationship endurance.

Permanence of Loss: This involves re-categorization of "no longer familiar, emotionally-active relevance" within consciousness as an executable cognitive efficiency. It shifts neuronal junctures as biological consciousness caps endurance with finality, recognizing what is non-recreatable and non-ressurectable emotively.

Permanence structurally maintains active, emotive connotations within consciousness. The emotive construct continuously evolves from the initial first-time meeting or exposure, creating a first impression that develops into a biological emotive characterization, which broadens introspectively through repeated exposures, third-party associations, and logic-associative processing, such as the smell of someone you know on another person. *Permanence* allows the exercise of a global memory structure that encompasses long-term emotional memory (of the subject) and conflates through to short-term memory. Correlation evolves breadth, contextualizing an aggregate of relevant memory structures.

Both *Permanence* and *Permanence of Loss* function as assistants to, not with, all memory structures and are globally interdependent within each individual, sustaining idiomatic-mapping contexts. For your dog's comprehension, whether it's a sibling or a foster dog's "disappearance," grief behavior may occur due to your dog's unfamiliarity with cogently introspecting "Where are they?" and "When are they coming home?"

Though when fosters depart your home, your dogs are not grieved or aggrieved concerning your feelings about the departure of the foster (or even their death).

In multi-dog families, however, when a beloved individual dies, parents often remark on the sadness they see in their surviving dogs after the "Goodbye."

We often incorrectly address our dogs' sadness through our human-centric, anthropomorphic conjecture by giving incidental consideration. Yet grief behavior is experienced the same in all familial-species.[53] Note that the length of time spent together doesn't necessarily create *permanence* endurance; rather it predicates upon emotional value (in relation to time-processing). Fostering is an educational opportunity to teach your dogs that departure is manageable, as the grief experienced is less than felt through the loss of a loved one, idiomatically contextualizing with consciousnessly processing *time*.

Death, however, is learnable through direct repetition, which reinforces the finality of life. For example, letting your other dogs visit and smell the body of their deceased sibling or human. Chemical decomposition is not immediately understood as proof of death, since the unfamiliar (for domesticated animals) strident body odor must be processed alongside motionlessness, lack of reciprocated interaction, and other cues.

The grieving individual's deductive reasoning may lack relevant context; yet the *memory structure* constructively supports their conclusion, despite the argument's obtuse and abstract nature.

Pain of Death

Death is represented through two distinct structures, with only one being learnable. The first is egocentric, driven by evolutional awareness of being injured by a predator. This scenario is not an understanding of death driving abject fear, but rather the visceral cogency of anticipating *intense* physical and psychological pain from the attacker. Animals don't comprehend dying. Animals fear psychologically, then upon interaction is the awareness that intense pain *will* happen. Everyone fears vicious pain. Death isn't introspectively or introvertively conceivable in such circumstances. Self-mortality is unteachable first-knowledge, which is why no dog wants to be *behaviorally euthanized* or suicided-by-human. Yet, the intense psychological fear endured caused by such academic killing is reprehensible.

The first *human* to witness their brethren killed or to come across a dead human body would have no idea what was wrong, only hoping that awakening might occur. After several days, cogency concludes that

[53] http://bit.ly/3VmN3m2

something had happened. Only the human-specie thinks of dying, because they understand and bi-communicate mortality through direct first-hand witnessing of another's death, which causes reflective context and formal articulation. We create the concept as the result of cogent logic.

Animals cannot, because no concept of repetitive death can be conveyed through any form of articulation to create societal awareness.

> *"Where's Grandma? Where did Grandma go?*
>
> *Will Grandma come back? When can I see Grandma again?*
>
> *What happened to Grandma?"*

The second structure of death for dogs pertains to the passing of another, similar to how a young child grapples with the concept of death. It extends beyond the psychological structures of *Permanence* and *Permanence of Loss*. An exclusively learned comprehension is something that doesn't evolve naturally but is acquired through experiences and exposure that contextualize the physical, cognitive, and egocentric circumstances.

Just as a curious toddler repeatedly asks about grandma and tries to grasp the elusive concept of death, dogs also need exposure to multiple instances of living creatures passing away during their lifetime to build a repeated structure of learning and comprehension, as well as interacting with the body–smelling, nosing, and touching. It is somewhat akin to transactive cadaver dogs, but the learning is given time to emotionally influence the cogency of the experience for aggregative conflation.

In essence, it's akin to teaching any individual a performative trick. Without repeated exposure and experiences, dogs may not fully grasp the concept of death as humans do. The understanding is intricately tied to one's life experiences and the lessons learned from the world around them. It's a testament to the importance of the role of companions and educators, who serve as human surrogate parents, guiding each dog through the profound intricacies of life and, eventually, the concepts and acts of death.

Human consciousness, by contrast, introspectively knows it *will* die. Other familial-species lack this awareness because they do not possess the same capacity for complex fantastical ideation, nor the depth of introspective egoselfishness that defines the human-specie.

Pawing

What may seem like a fascinating form of communication is actually your dog's articulate desire to engage independently with you. Your dog seeks emotional intimacy. The relationship isn't viewed as a partnership or "best friendship" due to the inherent familial intra- and co-dependent structure. You care for, feed, and guide your dog with the same care and affection you would give a child. Your dog's perception doesn't stem from infatuation or gratitude since the status quo for your dog isn't repeatedly insistent structurally.

Dogs are astute observers; they watch our hands in action–grasping objects from shelves, opening closed doors, preparing food for them, exchanging items with other humans, holding hands in affection, or offering consoling hugs similar to reset-hugs. Our hands engage in expressive gestures.

Dogs understand the self-control of their own legs and paw movements. Each claw can move independently, like fingers, albeit slightly and not dexterously. Dogs understand that human hands exhibit a broad spectrum of behaviors–actions that directly reflect control, intent, and emotional correlation are conveyed, whether loving or abusive. These are internalized through introspection and problem-solving via introvertive relevance.

When your dog paws at you, it is cogency: a deliberate attempt to solicit greater intimate affection from you–an overt, physical effort to communicate with you at a higher level of emotional processing, uniquely individual. At all times, your hands satiate your dog's craving to be acknowledged. This is not merely "reflective of consciousness"; it's a fully comprehended ego-selfish decisiveness, seeking greater consistent codependency with you. It's knowledge of cause and effect.

Pawing nurtures a sense of intensely important dependency within your dog's cross-species intradependency with you–a form of blossomed dependency initiated solely by your dog. It is autonomously decisive. Your dog's emotional inclusion hinges on their ability to communicate physically with you, shaped by observation and conclusive calculation to satiate the *need* to address your dog's loneliness. Pawing reflects your dog's strong intelligence due to causational experimentation.

If and when your dog seeks you by pawing, leaning against you, or seeking physical affection such as reset-hugs, these are all expressions of your dog's self-awareness. The emotional cognizance of feeling "a million miles away" is consciousnessly bridged through the intimacy of affection. This cogency is physically reconciled and quantified purely by your dog, not human-consequential behavior. Pawing quantifies consciousness through the demonstration of your dog's intricately complex intelligence. Pawing is a reflection of charisma.

I don't teach performative tricks like sitting, shaking paws, or fetching. Instead, when David approaches me, towering above my head and extends his paw, he is directly, overtly expressing his feelings, which are borne from his introspective self-awareness and objectification of himself and me. David could easily nuzzle his giant face into mine to get my direct attention. His development of empathy is further matured with my reciprocating acknowledgement and, thereby, validation of him as an individual. This signifies David's maturation, both in terms of dependency and maturing his awareness.

Keep in mind that pawing is not as prevalent in big and giant dogs for obvious reasons.

Your dog's message is clear: "I'm here, and I want to connect. I want to feel safe, protected, and loved." It's a beautiful testament to the depth of connection and communication that exists between humans and our beloved dogs in a contextually familial structure, transcending the boundaries of language with emotional resonance.

Your Dog Looks to You While Pooping

Have you ever wondered why your dog looks at you and then glances away while doing their business? Dogs do this because they're watching if you're keeping them safe during an extremely vulnerable circumstance. They are asking: *are you alert? Are you watching "our" environment?* Going to the bathroom is physically risky–it compromises their posture, slows their readiness, exposes them to potential threats, and physically retards response to danger.

When your dog feels confident that you're scanning the area, they process this as your familial protection of them. They will shift their gaze elsewhere to monitor areas where you are not watching, always keeping you within their peripheral vision. This is an evolutionary behavior designed to ensure familial safety despite being profoundly vulnerable.

That's why I stand firmly in place—feet planted, not moving even an inch—whether on the sidewalk, a trail, or a path, using either a regular or retractable leash. I remain still and intentionally look around: forward and backward, like with Loki,[54] and using my VoiceKey1 cues: "(Name), you're okay," or "(Name), go bathroom." By actively scanning the surroundings, I'm proving to my dog that I'm watching out for us. I literally predict Loki will look forwards and back, and explain the reason why in real time. Abandonment is foundate.

In this way, I step into the role of my dog's surrogate parent, offering protection and security. My dog, acutely aware of their own physical and sensory limitations in such a vulnerable state, depends on my steadiness and vigilance to sustain our shared sense of familial safety. Analogy: you're on a long drive with a friend, and you have to stop to use the bathroom. You would likely ask them to keep an eye out for approaching traffic so they can alert you if someone comes by while you're in a vulnerable position. That vulnerability stems from an emotionally-predicated *reality* and is not *self-conscious embarrassment*. You trust your friend implicitly.

This is analogous to how dogs feel unsafe when going to the bathroom, especially in unfamiliar locations. This results in a dog who doesn't go to the bathroom during an entire walk but will readily relieve themselves once near home, inside the home, in the yard, or in an area that feels secure and familiar.

If you use VoiceKey1—the protective reset-hug phrases—while standing still and deliberately scanning (sides and behind you, with your dog facing you), your dog will begin to check behind themselves as well. This stems from their awareness of vulnerability and their reliance on you, their surrogate parent, for consistent, familial protection at *all* times.

By intentionally looking toward each "corner" of the environment and speaking your dog's name with the correct VoiceKey phrasing, you demonstrate active vigilance across their entire perceptual range, including areas of dysfunction. This reinforces your dog's sense of self-objectification and dimensional objectification. Failure to do so aggregates into traits that become dysfunctional due to chronic *distrust* of their human parent.

---

[54] Arf Arf Bark Bark Rescue & Rehab, "Skittish Dog Training - @1 min I predict dog turns head forward & backwards. And why., *YouTube*, posted February 7, 2018, https://www.youtube.com/watch?v=iDP8fV1ETNk&t=63s

When your dog finishes going to the bathroom, remain standing in place. This demonstrates to your dog that you acknowledge the act as an extremely vulnerable moment for them. By choosing that specific spot, your dog made a decision about safety—and you're confirming it was a good one.

Loitering in the same place for about forty-five seconds allows your dog to introspectively confirm that their choice of location was safe. It also communicates that you trust their decision.

Dependency: Lessons in Trust

Building trust, especially with predatory dogs, requires the same foundational predicates as with abused dogs. It is monumentally imperative to apply parenting protocols consistently. How Nero learned to trust me, and eventually the public, required insights into the intricate rehabilitating of complex backgrounds.

Nero's story is a poignant reminder that a cogent comprehension of one's surroundings can create feelings of familial protection—or, conversely, abandonment and defenselessness. Nero's unique journey toward trust and understanding is a testament to the intricate nature of consciousness in familial-species and the profound impact of nurturing their life experiences.

Nero's history, marred by deeply troubling incidents, speaks to the core of his defense mechanisms, shaped by significant human abuse and willful abandonment. For Nero to comprehend his safety, I was obligated to protect him and not hurt him. While gradually teaching Nero to enjoy physical, non-violent touch, there were frequent times he would suddenly attack (not bite).

I'm disaggregating and destructuring Nero's "sudden snapping" to figure out possible reasons why. As I work to touch below his neckline, I'm prepared for what might happen in the event of his perceived retaliation. I didn't behave the way everyone else does when bitten. I maintain familial protection, which evolves my role as a human surrogate parent to Nero. Nero's familial reliance grows from the knowledge of being protected, safe, wanted (intra/co-dependencies), and emotionally reciprocated.

By understanding Nero's feelings of never having been protected, of living outside, and of being forced to defend himself against his fantastical-ideated sense of abandonment and defenselessness. In Alabama, a senior Great

Dane, emaciated on a prong collar and heavy chain, the psychogenesis of Nero's severe dysfunctional behaviors understandably unfolded the way they did. Nero didn't drag the woman off the couch to kill her because he was protecting the home; he dragged her onto the floor to gain a better position to try to kill her. If his intent had truly been "protection," he would have jumped onto the couch and attacked immediately.

By understanding Nero's feelings of never having been protected, of living outside, and of being forced to defend himself against his fantastical-ideated sense of abandonment and defenselessness, the psychogenesis of his severe dysfunctional behaviors understandably unfolded the way they did. Teaching Nero to trust, especially after such a traumatic and predatory history, was a transformative journey. It wasn't merely about Nero learning to trust any human—it was about him learning to trust me as his protector. A parent who would shield Nero from harm and finally provide the familial safety he had been denied his entire lonely utiliarian life.

Predation is introspectively managed—a testament to the profound transformations that trust and compassion bring. It serves as a poignant reminder that, just as a parent does for a child, familial dedication and commitment to Nero's well-being reshaped his world. This provided Nero with the healthy intradependency he had never known but fully comprehended, allowing him to experience a richly emotive and social life for three and a half years until the age of his passing at thirteen years, seven months, and one week.

My journey with Nero[55] is a powerful example of the healing and transformation that can exist within all healthy, intradependent relationships. With patience, understanding, and compassion, we can help all dysfunctional dogs, no matter their profound severity, find a sense of security and trust in the world. Though Nero profoundly exceeded the world's aggregated academia, he likely would have been killed out of inept ignorance and inexperience.

---

[55] Arf Arf Bark Bark Rescue & Rehab, "Nero," *YouTube*, posted September 9, 2019, https://www.youtube.com/watch?v=zoXfEGx9zgg.

Intimacy of Physical Affection

Your dog's response to physical contact, such as reset-hugs, can reveal a lot about their emotional state and individual sense of self. In this section, we'll explore the various circumstances that dogs may have when it comes to physical touch, such as a reset-hug, and what it signifies:

1. **The Term *Fear-Based Response* Reflects Professional Inexperience**
   When a dog avoids or immediately bolts away from a hug, that's rooted in their unfamiliarity with your actions and their emotive maturity and physical comfort. This is attributable to past negative experiences or dysfunctional intimacy-of-affection. If your dog allows a reset-hug for only a few seconds and then suddenly wants to get away, one reason is that your dog wants the affection, but introspectively, they aren't prepared to receive a heightened level of affectionate intimacy from you. During your dog's reset-hug, they'll feel highly complex foreign emotives surfacing while also enjoying your reset-hug; this is due to the complexity of sustained affection exceeding your dog's level of cogent familiarity with complex emotions. Your dog doesn't know how to process and needs to physically stop the new emotive complexity from continuing (defense, *then* offense). It's crucial to recognize that some dogs are inherently more sensitive to physical contact due to their unfamiliarity with experiencing complex affection or past abuse. They may initially perceive reset-hugs as uncomfortable rather than a loving, familial gesture—literally from "attack all humans and animals" to maturing into "lovingly huggable," as with Nero, Walter, David, and Andrew. Assuming this is a "fear-based response" is failing to comprehend "the forest and the trees." Behavior is nuanced due to introvertive objectification.

2. **Mental Trauma**
   Dogs and humans experience emotional trauma at a corresponding dilutive scale. If your dog has a history of being abused or subjected to frightening encounters, they may strongly resist physical contact. The sensitivity level of reset-hugs and esteemed patience is vital when dealing with dysfunctional dogs, especially at the level of predation. Your visceral evolution becomes significantly higher due to the complexity involved.

These sensitivities don't only surface in moments of direct human interaction but also in everyday environments. For example, dysfunctions like fear of fireworks must be approached with the same patience and awareness. With Mingki—who has been with me for just two months—I reassure him by showing that I too am alert to the very loud booms.

3. **Emotional and Lack of Dependency Response**
   If your dog isn't used to the reset-hug's intimate level of sustained affection, the *pulling away* is cogently deciding not to default to their core default emotive of rage and instead to ego-selfishly physically pull away from the cause of their emotional discomfort—a self-consciousness discomfort of prolonged physical contact, with the appearance of psychological apathy. Dogs have unique, individual idiosyncrasies that comprise their personalities, and just like people, some rightly have a dysfunctional view of the safety of their personal space due to abuse, etc. This doesn't mean they don't love their human parents, but rather highlights the criticality of building a healthily dependent, emotionally cogent dog.

4. **Seeking Human Contact**
   Dogs and humans are socially familial animals. Seeking human contact and affection isn't *dog-exclusive*; familial-species congruently appreciate affection. Humans have superior dexterity, with incomparable fine and gross motor control, making physically affectionate contact with other species profoundly comprehensible. Our dogs can't talk humanly. The sensations of being touched by humans are exquisite for familial-species. For a dog that has been physically abused, however, touch is entirely a direct risk of unknown personal injury from the human ("flight, THEN fight"). Such a dog may approach for things like belly rubs—a remnant of their puppyhood when they were cleaned and tongue-washed—but suddenly get up and leave to be by themself. These actions consistently reflect your dog's desire for connection, affection, and social interaction despite emotional difficulties being experienced.

   There are times when a dysfunctional dog receives a reset-hug. They may start to move their chest somewhat tensely (though not actually breathing tensely) **or** seem fine, only to immediately panic. This is intimacy-of-affection dysfunction, where the experiences begin saturation from an overload of complex emotions. Sensitivity is heightened, especially in dogs from abusive homes where they were physically beaten.

Some dogs with severe dysfunctions love receiving belly rubs and superficial affection just like a "normal, happy dog," but when given a proper reset-hug, they may panic and possibly bite. This is due to overwhelming feelings from foreign emotives exceeding their current threshold for processing complex familial intimacy. In other words, the emotional feelings and emotive structures from reset-hugging exceed your dog's emotional familiarity. This is often miscomprehended as *overwhelming*, *overloading*, *flooding*, or eustress, which reflects dog experts' inexperience working at the highly functional level required for rehabilitating predation.

5. **Variation in Behavior**
   It's important to remember that dogs vary in their responses to physical touch consequentially. For some dysfunctional dogs, the level of trust is significantly impaired. Building *trust* to the point of accepting a full reset-hug is fully attainable, but dog parents must be consistent and patient. Mingki, for example, is at the top of the dysfunction spectrum, with profound ancillary dysfunctions. Feral and justifiably extremely afraid of humans. I'm constantly determining the fine line in rehabilitation gain, day by day, in incremental slivers of progress that sometimes don't even amount to one percent progress over an entire week. In human circumstances, many individuals take years, even decades, to recover from their dysfunctions, even with professional counseling.

   When a dog has been traumatized by an abusive human parent, their logical, natural default is to stereotype all humans as a dangerous specie. What one dog may love, another may find uncomfortable due to the impacted level of familial trust. Take Walter, for example. When I first approached to give him a reset-hug, he would immediately attack me. Over time, his response shifted from attacking to biting. Sometimes, Walter would slowly stalk me; the fact that he was almost at my eyeline made it all the more frightening. This happened indoors and outdoors. Walter's history of significant, chronic, prolonged abuses had taught him that human contact eventually meant being beaten for normal behaviors that happened to upset his "owner" to beating him. Walter would slowly walk **at** me, knowing he could easily catch me. His high-functioning cogency of both his parameters and mine, exemplified his charismatic cogency.

Understanding your dog's individual preferences and level of emotional maturation is key to nurturing a positive and loving relationship where your dog isn't trying to escape your embrace due to a lack of trust in you. In the event of an emergency or fight, it's imperative that your dog is cogently familiar with experiencing extremely complex foreign emotives in urgent or violent circumstances so as to reduce the chance of you being bitten inadvertently to a day where your dog actively seeks long, enduring reset-hugs from you for your genuine familial safety.

For example, Walter went from stalking me during our initial weeks to receiving full, long reset-hugs, from me, even when he was angry or had a fight. He would come to me for physical protection or emotional comfort immediately after a significant confrontation. There would be times when Walter would get angry at home—at me or at another dog. The first thing I would do was talk to him using the same simple lexicon with VoiceKey, consistently, from the beginning to the end of our life together. Walter eventually learned how to come to me on his own. Still, he would then quickly walk away, self-consciousness about seeking a human safe harbor. Later, during partial rehabilitation, Walter would walk away but return to pace near me, trying to reconcile the immense emotional and psychological contradiction he recognizes congruently. Finally, through full rehabilitation, Walter learned to trust my protection.

At that time, Walter would stay for the entire reset-hug duration—even when highly emotionally confronted. I would ask him (not call or demand) to come to me for a reset-hug. In the beginning, Walter wouldn't come to me, which stems from human distrust due to his abused experiences. His thought process was essentially: *"I just did something wrong, and now my human parent wants me to come to them so they can continue to yell or hurt me."* Sadly, this is normal for the majority of abused dogs.

I had to teach Walter that I wasn't angry, but instead providing consistent familial protection—the same protection he received during all "normal" times in our family-group, even if he has bitten me significantly.

> Walter's example follows the exact same approach, behaviors, and actions that were equally manifested by Lincoln Sr., Nero, Lincoln Jr., William, David, Johnathon, Mingki, and every client's dog that I have worked with, resulting in precisely the same successful rehabilitation.

In summary, while most dogs will enthusiastically welcome hugs and physical affection, others may initially be indifferent. Some may be significantly negative to such intimacy of affection due to past trauma, personality, or dysfunctional individual boundaries. Recognizing and respecting your dysfunctional dog's emotional needs–and the initial narrowness of their physical boundaries due to a lack of familial protection–is critical. Historically aggregated and conflated context is fundamental in building your autodidactic education and becoming a trusted human parent. It's essential to anthropomorphize your intuition to foster a strong and trusting parental bond with your dog. As dog parents, it's **our responsibility** to ensure that our dog feels loved, safe, and respected in our daily familial interactions with them.

The harm is that "modern science" dog training and "evidence-based" dog experts continue to cause by their naive inexperience is believing that they're even a smidgen close to developing an empirical "science-based, psychologically sound" approach. Modern science's killing rate has only increased due to profound academic ineptitude and arrogance.

The Progress of Healing

Severely abused dogs like Walter don't live long due to *behavioral euthanasia* because academia can't comprehend profound dysfunction. Next, the physiological taxation shortens lifespans. To undergo his unique journey of rehabilitation, shedding light requires an understanding of the resilience of cogent familial-species navigating the world of emotions without egotistical self-interest. Achieving tiny incremental milestones in progress is essential to note and acknowledge, as it supports a dysfunctional dog on their path to successful rehabilitation. Intuiting behavior into sensible notations of quantification means traversing the ever-changing gradient of dysfunction toward rehabilitation, which becomes tangible and realistic–one tiny step at a time.

Walter embarked on a journey of recovery that spanned an entire lifetime, one that should have been filled with distinct milestones of beneficial, visceral consciousness development. Being subjected to repeated, frequently severe abuse and neglect relentlessly oppressively retarded his capacity for healthy emotive maturation. Rehabilitating Walter meant that he would learn his visceral milestones in a multitude of circumstances during his adulthood with me. Instead of being represented through puppyhood pedantically, Walter's experiences weren't gradual or transitional.

Checking My Location

Walter's progress continued immensely as he realized he enjoyed checking in with me, seeking reassurance and safety from his newfound guardian–a parental beacon away from the darkness of his past.

Running JETSAI SuperCar Transport, I would often fall asleep on the couch at night after coming home. Walter would come out of the bedroom to check on me. Since he was off-leash and free to roam the house, it was only natural that I feared being attacked while sleeping. When Walter first arrived, I even encircled my bed with makeshift fencing, just in case. I was extremely scared.

So when I fell asleep on the couch, I would wake up to the sound of Walter's distinctive 183-pound footsteps on the wood floor. If I heard him in time, I would cover my head except for my eyes, so I could covertly watch him–but unlike in the bedroom, I didn't have the safety of makeshift fencing in the living room. I'd pretend to be asleep.

Walter would walk through the room, stopping to locate me visually, and then he would walk back to the bedroom where Nero and Sammie were sleeping. Walter wasn't "protecting." He was wondering why I was not in the bedroom. This isn't herding. It's familial intradependency driving Walter's need to find me. Nero and Sammie were still incidental to Walter's familial context, as he was still new to everyone. Walter was looking for me to self-soothe his healing from familial abandonment. As Walter became braver, he would approach me for awkward affection. Walter and I were very afraid of each other.

Walter would gently sniff my entire body, hidden under the blanket, the first time he checked in. Subsequently, Walter knew it was me, visually shaped. He would walk up to my "sleeping body" and sniff my exposed face only. He could see and smell that it was me, but he needed to confirm that it was indeed me, not because of OCD, but self-reassurance. Sometimes, I would "wake up," and Walter and I would have an amicable engagement, being mindful of the environment if it was dark–since it was very dangerous with

Walter due to his impaired vision, hearing, and significant abuse history. I would calm myself and say his name with VoiceKey1, just as I normally would when talking with him.

After a while, Walter would stay with me and sleep on the couch beside me. Sometimes, Walter would go back to the bedroom to join Nero and Sammie. The familial value of societal integration was important for Walter to learn that he is equally important and emotionally included within our family.

Being observant and positioning myself closer to Walter during off-leash park visits, I would say his name with a familial tone and constantly. I'm not at the dog park to socialize for myself–if I'm blabbering to someone, I'm distracted from parenting Walter. By frequently communicating with Walter, I let him know that I was acknowledging his location and circumstances as he actively explored the park. I would do the same at home and during car rides. The connection provided Walter with a way to show him that we're together as a family, regardless of the circumstances. Using his name acknowledged Walter as an individual while further defining his idiomatic relevance by enriching the complexity of his self-objectification.

Walter would seek me out first whenever he felt scared, alone, unacknowledged and insecure. At first, Walter would look in my direction, and I would call him to give him a reset-hug: "Walter, come here" and "Walter, give me a hug." I would escalate my communications *slowly* if Walter is walking toward me or he's walking away from a threatening circumstance that he couldn't emotively process. When Walter came directly to me, he was blatantly quantifying nonverbal bi-communication that he needed from me to give him a reset-hug. To make him feel safe.

Walter's story is a testament to the resilience of animal cogency and the transformative power of understanding and patience. Walter arrived with a harrowing history due to his traumatic past of abuse and violence.

To truly appreciate Walter's remarkable transformation and the stages he navigated, I highly recommend reading his description and watching the video *Walter and the Bear.*[56] It shows both his dysfunctions and his ability to

---

[56] Arf Arf Bark Bark Rescue & Rehab, "Walter and the Bear," *YouTube*, posted January 9, 2020, https://www.youtube.com/watch?v=2Sx5cWYukDI

cogently self-regulate significant dysfunctions of an asset. His story sheds light on my empirical work on rehabilitating predation.

Walter's journey is a shining example of how, with unwavering dedication and an understanding of the actual intricacies of behavior and consciousness, we move beyond our assumption of demarcative consciousness. All sophisticated life functions are, in fact, "self-aware of their emotional context." For animals that cannot idiomatically contextualize their experienced emotions, the default is to return to their core emotives. Rehabilitation requires the cogent processing of complex foreign emotions in relation to the familial construct. No amount of "modern science" or "evidence-based" dogma can refute the empirical success of my work. Even the most severely traumatized, abused dogs shall find hope, healing, and a chance at a new life when we comprehend that we possess sophisticated anthropomorphic intuition to downtrain, stabilize, and rehabilitate all dysfunctions.

CHAPTER 12

Understanding Dog Behavior: A Psychological Analysis

A Window Into the Canine Psyche

At the old rancher, we were blessed with a spacious, fully fenced quarter-acre backyard. At its center stood an eighty-foot-tall tree, making it a true paradise–a place where everyone played. When boredom struck, they would gather at the door, patiently waiting to come inside or occasionally lounge on the doggy beds. Walter, being the massive boy he was, would sprawl across one bed–his front paws dangling off the edge, his rear end hanging over the back.

Nero (r) and Walter at the rancher.

I worked from home, and it became a familiar routine for everyone to hang out in whichever room I was in. Familial-species rely on shared codependency to stay close, a testament to unwavering comprehension and emotional desire for family. Walter would sometimes approach me when I was working on my laptop; his height meant his head was above mine, nose sniffing about, seeking affection. Walter was feeling lonely.

Walter's approach wasn't solely about affection; he cogently made an effort to engage further—an intradependent connection with me. Walter would amble around, curiously sniffing various mundane objects near me, eventually coming face-to-face with me. His history of severe abuse and various abandonments made him self-concerned while seeking my affection. Deep down, Walter feared: *what if I spurned him, just like so many previous families?*

Walter comprehended rejection viscerally. It wasn't his history of beatings and abuse making him reluctant to approach me—it was his awareness that others had shunned him, not out of cruelty, but out of fear of being attacked.

Walter worried about "the other shoe dropping," bracing for the moment I might reject him. This affected his self-esteem, worried about being yelled at or physically forced away, contributing fulsomeness to Walter's predacious dysfunction.

Every domesticated dog, from birth through puppyhood, is carried like an infant—bonded in tacit intradependence. One day, the puppy grows too big to carry. That change is often processed as rejection, affecting self-worth. For Walter, these compounded experiences degraded his sense of familial inclusion. This was not a "fear period."

Not receiving respectful acknowledgment from me causes Walter's self-withdrawal—what I call self-marginalization—suffusing and entrenching his overall dysfunctions, furthering his introvertive, isolative structure. This commonality often occurs in children, who frequently exhibit unintended belligerence.

For example, if your dog is lounging on the couch and suddenly goes to the kitchen, they're often following their stomach. This is overt, indirect physical communication—asking you for food. When you get hungry, you can make yourself a snack without having to ask anyone. As a child, however, you rely on your mom or dad. Your dog has no such option. They depend on you, and they also know you don't always respond consistently. Sometimes it's because you don't want to, but more often, it's because you're not noticing their nonverbal bi-communication.

Caveat: Iwis academia shall forever struggle to understand Walter's behavior (behaviorism can't comprehend), as psychosomatic expressions—an alternative strategy of indirect communication designed to seek my affection. This points to a highly sophisticated consciousness, rooted in Walter's sophisticated emotive awareness and achieved through the strategic execution of complex cogency.

Dogs, in fact, are imbued with sophisticated emotional complexity. Their behavior consciousnessly reflects thoughts along the lines of: *"I'm lonely, and I'm not sure how to ask for affection."* The brain contextualizes this to reference similar circumstances in an individual's memory of resultant cause-and-effect comparatives, which surfaces a larger context of emotive memory, albeit immature sophistication–an introspective salient attempt to idiomatically correlate and conflate ego-selfish problem-solving.

This is represented similarly in a child who asks its parent for a snack while snuggled up beside them. In the same way, your dog's psychological understanding of hunger is layered–it isn't defined solely by the severity of physical hunger, but by how familial-species process pain and need. Dogs compartmentalize different aspects of pain, but true psychological comprehension does not endure to become a consistent behavioral pattern unless the circumstance is endured by repetition (such as repetitive starvation). This is part of the larger introspection structure.

Walter, however, didn't follow that pattern. His self-objectification continued to richly evolve despite the abuses he had endured, elevated by each home. Giant dogs are more severely abused simply because of their size, and Walter bore the weight of that reality. Yet Walter learned that articulating his feelings negatively toward me–through his attacks, for example–would not result in beatings, yelling, or my disingenuous "behaving" thereafter. Instead, Walter came directly to me, without the fear of the old repercussions. His comprehension of contrasting circumstances illustrates the intricacies of his cogency. If Walter were hungry, he would naturally head for the kitchen. But when Walter wanted to engage with me, he would make a deliberate beeline for my presence.

As much as ineptitude causes the needless killing of predatory dogs, it's another profound loss for academia, as it presents an opportunity to learn much more about predation from an epitome of evolved consciousness at the fulsome apex of complexity in sentience. Predatory dogs exhibit significant self-awareness, cogent maturation, and the presence of substantial psychological processing. In other words, a unique trait of predatory dogs is their high charisma, intrinsic to their profound dysfunctions. The complexity of being predacious or *vicious* isn't due to rage or "typical animalism."

Predatory dogs are not misanthropic, even when scarred by lifetimes of human abuse. Nero, Walter, and other predatory giants didn't seek my attention, affection, and love to please me, or that I was "different from all the others." Trust was forged through action, words, and my assurance of genuine familial belonging. The idea that dogs exist in a default state of perpetual happiness–always open, submissive, or eager to love–is a profound misrepresentation of the reality of all familial-species.

When we moved to the new house, I anticipated that Walter and the others would stay unusually close. They feared abandonment or some unseen threat, unsettled by an unfamiliar environment where every room felt strange and unsafe. Much like children clinging to their parents when visiting an unfamiliar home, Nero, Walter, and the rest of our family group needed time–and assurance–to process why all our belongings were in a new place, and why we were staying there overnight. It was a new yet "unsafe place."

It's like being a child scared of your parents' attic because you thought there were ghosts, monsters, and other scary ideations. You tell your parents about it, and one day, they bring you upstairs and show you that it's safe and that there's nothing to be scared about. Days later, the same attic transforms as your secret hideout, a place to store your treasures. The fear dissolves not because the attic changed, but because your parents acknowledged your concerns and walked you through the "unknown," turning it into your family's safe space.

Walter's dependency on me evolved as he experienced more complex and emotional structures. Experiencing complexity consciousnessly evolved Walter's cogency through emotional circumstantial familiarity. At times, Walter would saunter from the bedroom and rest his Great Dane head on my arms while I worked on my laptop at the dining table–a poignant display of his loneliness.

Through these times of increasing intimacy, initially, I had to quell my concerns that Walter would be overwhelmed by the stillness and complexity of the emotions he experienced so deeply, as he wanted to be physically near me because he felt safe. Yet, the very act of feeling lonely *before* leaving the bedroom hinted at his growing self-awareness and even a kind of fantastical ideation. For me, this was daunting as Walter's head towered above mine.

There were moments when these foreign emotions seemed to confuse and frighten Walter, and he misinterpreted their psychological weight as harm coming from me. In those moments, Walter would nip, bite or lunge at my face—emblems of his conflicted feelings—sometimes escalating into tense situations where he cornered me between the wall and table in a state of confused anger.

Walter's journey with me was filled with challenges—it marked profound moments of understanding, comprehension, and connection that ultimately enriched our bond as dog and parent.

Prey Drive, Predation, and Raw Meat

I've found that predation and prey drive are relatively simple dysfunctions to rehabilitate. *Predation* is a form of consumption that seemingly requires killing. Food is intrinsic from day one of life. Predation reflects significant cognition, analysis, and the circumstances and success thereof. Predation isn't sophisticated in complexity. It's logically efficient, task-driven, yet emotionally predicated.

Prey drive, on the other hand, is an evolutional interest and reflects the structure and evolution of velocity-targeting. It functions more as entertainment than survival, and it must be recognized as separate from predation.

Both are satiate primal cravings. Think of it like having a years-long craving for a favorite food. One reason I feed a raw meat diet is to address an intrinsic, evolutional craving for raw meat. The texture itself—masticating the very inheritance of predation—speaks to that deep, ancestral drive. A raw diet is a food that presents familial importance and not transactiveness, learning meat as a nutritious asset while answering evolutionary survival needs.

Familial-species control and self-regulate their anger and rage, in direct contradiction to the predation and prey drive that behaviorism claims can't be rehabilitated. It is the very foundation of sophisticated consciousness (default emotives). To put it simply, it is to control pure predation to emotionally cohabitate. Emotional control is cogent thereon. Domesticated dogs attacking over food are expressing severe socially negative interactions due to self-esteem dysfunction or food un-security. Feeding eight dangerous-to-predatory dogs raw organs, raw (uncooked) bones, and raw meat presents a significant anthropomorphic understanding of successful inter-relational familialships.

Gentle Collar Practices and Leash Use

Leash manners can be challenging for dog experts, especially for new intakes. With Great Danes, the challenge is magnified—they're extremely powerful. I often walked them through nature parks at 2 a.m., where we would encounter various wildlife, including coyotes, bears, and cougars.[57] Managing those moments required addressing both predation and prey-drive interest. One encounter, documented in a video[58] featuring William and David, shows the both of them remaining composed in the presence of coyotes, proving prey and extreme predation are cogently habilitated.

The detrimental impact of corrective dog collars is detrimental to your dog's well-being, and the damage is often ineptly underestimated by academia and politicians. Gentle collar practices, on the other hand, dismantles the lazy justification for prong, choke, or e-collars, proving that genuine, compassionate handling not only protects dogs but also improves their overall quality of life by further fostering familial kindness.

The most common—yet bizarre—equivocation for brute-force collars is: *"Prong collars don't hurt."* This exposes dog experts' ineptitude in comprehending how dogs process pain. Naively, they proselytize that dogs have a "very high pain tolerance" or that they don't process pain. It's illogical and naive not to comprehend that familial-species don't overtly show glaring signs of suffering or articulate their pain due to lack of idiomatic introspection, cause-and-effect and circumstantial context.

An immensely rude, disrespectful, and asinine claim: *"I've put on a prong collar on my own throat, and it didn't hurt!"* Prong collars are barbed, sharp metal spikes that concentrate all force into knitting needle-sized contact points against a dog's hypersensitive throat. A dog professional using a prong or e-collar is inexperienced in addressing dysfunctions as the use of a deliberately painful, brute-force device is a lazy approach that forces compliance. By contrast and by fact, a highly experienced dog expert only

---

[57] http://bit.ly/4mnx8iu

[58] Arf Arf Bark Bark Rescue & Rehab, "Coyotes? July 1, 2022," *YouTube*, posted July 11, 2022, https://www.youtube.com/watch?v=75zF_neQOOc

needs a basic fabric cinch or buckle collar and a basic six-foot lead. The only valid use of a slip-collar is to prevent a flight risk in cases where a dog might back out of a collar or harness while trying to run away.

It's impossible for any dog to "dominate the leash" because the human parent has dominant physical control of the leash, which circles back to the dog expert's inexperience. I openly challenge any trainer to put a "no pain" prong collar around their neck, attach it to someone holding a six-foot leash, and run full speed to the end. The result would be intense pain, drawn blood, and likely a severe sprain.

Hypersensitivity, flinch response, and high reception to pleasurable touch–yet conversely, pain does not exist? There is always a counter-position threshold as per evolutional construct; otherwise, humans and animals wouldn't exist due to unknowingly "boiling in hot water" as the frog, causing cessation of that specie's ability to apex-optimize their existence.

I use a basic collar and basic six-foot leash. Over time, however, I have taught myself to use retractable leashes proficiently. The learning curve wasn't without setbacks–I've fallen, been dragged, and made my share of mistakes. In all instances, I've realized, it was always my fault or a result of inattentiveness.

Retractable leashes are excellent for experienced users only. It teaches lateral cogency, recall without treats, and furthers developing inclusive familial contextualization idiomatically.

Walking with retractable leashes might seem unconventional to some. However, their current design can be greatly improved. Still, this technical tool provides profound opportunities for *lateral autonomy*.

With experience and skill, I have mastered walking Lincoln Jr. (170 pounds), William (160 pounds), and David (211 pounds) totaling over 540 pounds, with three retractable leashes with a single hand. This unique approach, which I showcase in these videos,[59] shows how full control can be maintained even with all three dogs lunging. This debunks criticism of retractable leashes, proving complaints are user error or ineptitude.

---

[59] Arf Arf Bark Bark Rescue & Rehab, "Retractable Leashes (Especially) With Dysfunctional Dogs Provide Circumstancial Cogency playlist," *YouTube*, https://www.youtube.com/playlist?list=PLK43vpl6h3zYDBe0dcpgjYFkpcgi-FSYc

My videos show me using **three** retractable leashes used at the same time with a single hand–and ambidextrously. I cognitively process each finger independently while holding the camera with my other hand for over an hour in my videos. Each of my fingers holds the massive weight of each dog individually and collectively. Is this impossible? Hardly. Rock climbers freehand climb entire cliffs, sometimes using only their fingertips, enduring variables like wind, momentum, and fatigue. Often, they carry their entire body weight and equipment with their fingertips, forcing leverage on their fingers and hands. By comparison, using separate fingers is 100 percent doable and doesn't make me unique.

They lunge when other dogs bark at us. Dogs dig into the ground, exerting two to three times their body weight. So, from a combined weight of 540 pounds, digging in with power sometimes exceeds 1,500 pounds, requiring individually controlling my own body mechanics and center of gravity.

Practice, practice, practice. That's required. It takes months to become proficient. A dog expert who doesn't know how to use a retractable leash has a miscomprehension of physics and hand-eye coordination when they complain. Whether using a basic collar with a six-foot lead or retractable leash, the skill lies not in the tool but in the handler's ability to downtrain, stabilize, and rehabilitate dogs–both dysfunctional and "normal." I've observed seven reasons dog trainers hate retractable leashes.[60]

1. They get easily frustrated.
2. They are impatient.
3. They are deficient in hand-and-eye coordination.
4. They are unable to "walk-and-chew gum at the same time."
5. They don't have hand and arm strength.
6. They are negligent; they don't pay attention.
7. They are scared of retractable leashes technical complexity.

Asset Protection

Determining the reason for *resource protection* predicates upon introvertive dysfunction. Why dogs protect assets is determined by deconstructing perceived threats and emotional vulnerabilities. Personal items, such as socks or underwear, have a significant familial scent concentration. Your dog's

[60] http://bit.ly/46MqZGB

interpretation of their own familial stability and emotional "safety blanket" to self-soothe their introvertive and abandonment issues. By taking intimate personal items of their human parent, a contrived sense of inclusive belonging within their family structure can lead to loneliness. Much like soldiers carrying tokens from loved ones into war, dogs lean on the trifecta of physical, visual, and psychological attachment that these items provide.

When a familial-specie(s) repeatedly takes personal items belonging to a particular person, this reflects a greater dysfunction: abandonment issues, fragile intradependency, and low self-confidence. The act is an attempt to artificially seek superficially higher emotional input to self-soothe emotional instability. They are not materialistic; instead, exhibiting low self-esteem, low self-confidence, and limited emotional maturity. Taking toys or household items reflects your dog's attempts to self-marginalize and occupy themselves despite being introspectively aware of their feelings of ostracism.

Certain objects carry specific meaning. Footwear, keys, or jackets are cues of departure; an individual recognizes these items as symbolic of being left behind, regardless of whether they're actually invited to go along.

Even odd items, like a TV remote, reflect an unsophisticated, emotive structure that feels displaced. Still, their level of psychological upset isn't dysfunctionally impairable. The fierceness of protection isn't as genuinely emotionally nuanced.

A sophisticated consciousness functions by emotionally objectifying the chosen item. Your dog's direct manifestation of introspective awareness is that they've made a cogent decision to expend physical effort to get up, retrieve the item, and bring it back to a place of safety. Their act of championing the item is analogous to someone at a sports game catching the winning ball thrown into the crowd. Having to protect from others who also want the ball. Viciousness surmounts, if not for immediate societal disapproval, yet it evolves Darwinistically. This bridges with animals' consciousness, recognizing *personal task* behavior, which evoloutionally predates *predation* both in motivation and conclusion. Driven by emotional and psychological intent, traits of egoselfishness and egocentrism are immature: "Therefore, I am."

As with Lincoln Jr., swallowing items or clothing will cause serious medical issues, which can result in major surgery. It happens when your dog ideates self-marginalization due to perceived abandonment, causing them to feel the need to isolate their dysfunctions with tenuously difficult, albeit ineffective attempts to self-soothe their limited emotional envelope. Consumption is a consequence, not an ancillary or typically deliberate act. Your dog's protective interest with a certain item or toy reflects a desire not to be alone. It seems contrarian, but the protection of toys, at a psychological level, is a form of introverted self-soothing.

Even if your dog protects toys from other dogs or humans, the outward aggression is often a facade for their underlying introversion. It's not "aggression," but rather immediate diplomacy within physical limitations for dogs to express. Protecting is superficial, even when it is food. If your dog protects food, it must be understood in the same frame as predation, prey drive, and Darwinism: food is not a transactional "high-value asset," but a familial constant.

Ensuring that food is not reduced to a materialistic transaction is important for a dog's cogency maturation. Food is a familial-established intradependency from the day of birth. Food is used for more than just survival; it's about beneficial connections. Food is considered a normal occurrence of being part of a family. Food is taught to children and animals as a symbol of familial inclusion–representing intimacy, protection, and safety. However, food can be controversial for dogs that are dysfunctional or starved, and care should always be exercised when trying to take a food item from an individual with whom you're not familiar. I have rehabilitated dogs whose food guarding has resulted in people requiring major surgery, even from something as simple as walking past them at mealtime.

Food and other assets require knowledge and proof that they'll be returned to your dog and have no fiat representation, such as bribery. Food is familial because it's exactly what occurs after birth, onward into maturation. To a dysfunctional dog, food is a symbol of safety. Perversion of food into a transaction reflects human impatience and insecurity, leading to a superficial relationship. I endeavor to give food without obligation, performance, or waiting, thus establishing food as a normal part of familial life.

Scale the type of asset being retained or protected to determine your dog's unique dysfunction correctly. Although expressions of various protectiveness by your dog may be intimidating, the fundamental reason for *food* is understandable as a sign of intimacy. It is similarly correlated with human behavior on a corresponding scale. Correctly anthropomorphizing intuition while recognizing evolutional survival sophistication for such significant idiomatic contextualization.

Behaviors should never be assumed or aligned as genericisms, nor assumed to be limited to a specific context. The mistakes of academia seek convenience by confluence and thus cratered academic intuition from disaggregating and destructuring deeper past the minutiae "innate."

I provide familially-protective supervision of all, equally. This consistency is imperative. Familial context is **not** a status of "leader to the subordinates"; it should be hierarchy by chronological birth, and for rescue dogs, hierarchy by chronological seniority. Nor applied as primogeniture. No "favorites." It's beneficial to recognize my family group by their arrival date, regardless of age.

Section I: The Canine Mind

Tail Wagging Is Introvertive Communicative

One of the most intriguing behavioral errors is the miscomprehension of tail behavior, sometimes termed *tail-set*. Tail behavior is highly contextualized body language that is introvertively founded–a consequential product of thinking. Self-awareness is richly ego-selfish. Regardless if your dog is alone or not, tail behavior quantifies objective self-awareness and introspective processing. Tail behavior manifests ego-selfish; introspective analysis. A scalable analogy: imagine being in an important meeting where one of your team members nervously shakes their knee. They are not "communicating" to you; they are revealing their own internal state of cogency disruption.

Musculature structure, rhythm, direction, and cadence are represented in *tail wagging*. It's not representative of two-way communication: each dog's process of consciousness manifests physically. Other tail-bearing familial-species comprehend tail behavior due to self-objective comprehension. For example, stories of one dog approaching another with their tail wagging high, only for a fight to break out, illustrate that tail movement is ego-selfish-driven behavior. If tails were truly a form of communication, there would be no *up-tail* negative interactions; evolution removes deficiencies in communication through attrition. Tail behavior refers to your dog's cognitive and emotional thought processes. Tail behavior indicates aspects of emotives within their surroundings. Tail musculature reflects cogent processing. Briefly:

Up-tail: Analytical and strategic processing of the immediate circumstance. Dogs weigh inputs for assimilation, recalling similar emotional or historical experiences. Indicates logical, deliberate cognition–not nervousness, not excitement. These details are explicit structures of consciousness.

Midway-tail: Actively introvertive and ego-selfishly aware. Dogs evaluate their circumstances through their own immediate perspective. Active understanding. Shows a heightened self-awareness and "consideration" of one's circumstance. Reflects active introspection.

Down-tail: Egocentric self-concern with gradience. Suggest worry–of loss, of self, of vulnerability. Represents introvertive self-preservation.

Long-term, then Short-term Memory

Understanding memory construction is essential because memory significantly shapes behavior. Dogs, like humans, rely on both short-term and long-term memory. Without memory, empathy could neither exist nor function. Long-term memory is developed, process-wise, by evolution; successive progeny iterations of a mnemonic individual. In this way, learned memory aggregates biologically–what we often call genetic heredity. Hence, *time* is ancillary.

Short-term memory requires a higher biological demand due to active reconciliatory processing, which occurs in an elliptical cycle. Constructional for consciousness–from short-term to long-term memory–requires anchoring memory in the physical biology by mapping it through emotive context. Emotions give memory long-term relevance and shape how familial-species perceive time due to idiomatic import.

Without short-term, evolving emotives can't provide sustained introspection. For short-term to migrate unto long-term storage, it requires emotive connotation regardless if negative or positive. The idiomatic contextualization relies upon the full spectrum of memory.

Societal Cogency ("Socialization")

Healthy socialization is essential for dogs to develop healthy interpersonal relationships. The ability to learn self-objectification maturates empathetic cogency. Introvertive evolves one's introspective. Using your dogs' names is imperative. Always "helicopter" your dog–stay physically close enough to calmly and very quickly intervene. Verbally check on how your dog's body movements appear to you. This reassurance allows dysfunctional dogs to feel safe enough to experience their complex emotive structure with their human parent immediately present to physically intervene or safely provide a reset-hug. Keep in mind that dogs interact face-to-face, most circumstances occur just inches apart–so perspective and scale are paramount to comprehending the intensity of physical interaction as more than just saying "hi."

Section II: Coping Mechanisms

Isolation and Seeking Comfort

Dogs cope with their dysfunctions in various ways, such as the "shy dog" who's always seeking isolation by way of self-marginalization. This often stems from self-esteem dysfunction caused by insufficient maturation and narrow emotional attachment. Familial emotions are gradually built day by day. Providing visceral comfort, as their human parent, often happens by using your dog's name. Think of the first time someone said your name while telling you, *"I love you."* The complexity of familial emotions aggregates from diverse yet simple learning structures, contextualizing across an extremely large idiomatic map.

Self-marginalization can become self-exiling. Withdrawing typically occurs with the chronologically senior dog; after dinner, they go to the bedroom alone or lies away from the main family area. This is most evident with multi-dog families. Self-marginalization can occur when a family inadvertently ignores their eldest child, which can negatively impact self-esteem, self-worth, and self-confidence. Objectification is confluent with self-awareness; this is empathetic awareness.

Physiological harm is a common condition in severely abused dogs. For example, Great Danes often develop stress-related heart issues, regardless of pedigree. Dysfunctions are created from intense emotional experiences, such as always being yelled at by a human parent. Psychological stress affects people as they age.

There will be times when your dog will go to another room or lay further away; these are deliberate, cogent executions of ideation-seeking and self-exiling intradependency, yet they are rhetorical cause-and-effect, especially if the human parent *doesn't* pick up on nonverbal physical bi-communication. If your dog is self-marginalizing, spend at least twenty minutes or more in that room with them, engaging in minimal physical interaction. This is helpful in rebuilding self-confidence and fostering familial inclusion. It's "watching the sunset together."

Part 6
Behavioral Study of Dogs

CHAPTER 13

Revolution of Dogs

Question of a Canine Soul

Preface: Just days after writing this chapter, my beloved David suddenly died from a heart attack. Stephen died from heart failure shortly after this past Christmas. I have lost seven beloved Great Danes in as many years and Aby's rescue recently let me know cancer took her life.

As a child, I often pondered the mysteries of the afterlife, uncertain whether my deeds would grant me passage through the pearly gates or condemn me to the fiery abyss. Is there an *"undiscovered country,"* as William Shakespeare prosed? Does our consciousness follow our Soul, or do both fade away forever?

The constant worry weighed on my mind. But amid this uncertainty, one thing remained unquestionably clear: I possessed a Soul. I knew I had a Soul because I feared the endlessness of death. As a child, I learned that conventional religion stated there was life after death. If there was, why didn't I intrinsically feel mortally safe? I felt mortality as a child. I knew that my deliberateness in everything I did was a result of my conscious planning and execution of my fantastical ideas. I knew that when I made a decision, whether it resulted in a positive or negative outcome, was a personal, free-willed choice based on analyzing my facts, emotions, and relative to the operation of my own psychology.

The question of whether dogs have Souls has ironically fascinated humanity for centuries despite the fatally erroneous claim centuries ago by religious leaders claiming *"No."* Pondering the existence of all Souls draws a corresponding dilutive scale amongst familial-species' consciousnesses. By contemplating the essence of a dog's being, we delve into the philosophical and metaphysical aspects of existence.

> *Life is not a right; life is succinctly a privilege. Whether one human lives or dies is an arbitrary decision relative to the grand consideration of evolution and the billions of humans of its specie.*

"Dogs possess Souls."

This simple statement stirs deep contemplation. My response is yes.

Dogs, humans and familial-species exhibit autonomous emotive process structures. They experience a pleasure-to-pain spectrum. Familial-species begin their love without conditions–but unlike humans, with lessened materialist predation. Their capacity for sophisticated consciousness is undeniable. It's a reminder that the thresholds of consciousness extend beyond the human-specie realm, demonstrating that familial-species possess complex empathy. Recognizing functional sentient consciousness in dogs, we acknowledge the richness of their emotional world. The depth of dogs' cogent experiences forges stronger connections between our familial-species beyond emotive isomorphistic cohabitation. Our long history of shared evolution is evidence of this, even against the backdrop of human cruelty–whether through barbaric treatment of dogs, the torture and consumption of "meatdogs," or the wasteful exploitation of other familial-species we reduce to "meat-farm animals." This is apocalyptical for human-specie evolution.

Do degrees of biological species complexity, displayed with illustrious sophistication of self-awareness, therefore qualify to surpass an arbitrary threshold quantification to qualify for such exclusive, demarcated membership? Is humanity's claim to exclusive ownership of the "biological Soul" be justified merely because the human-specie can build, talk, introspect, objectify, and empathize with our version of *sophisticated consciousness*?

What, then, is a dog with a Soul? Do we cajole the courts and judges for their failure to draw upon their maturity and breach the confines of their reticent comforts and timidity to correctly afford limited legal rights to dogs as functional sentient beings? Ergo, "Soul" afforded by legal decree? If by doing so, does the harsh light of killing tens of millions of "psychologically distressed dogs" in North America stand as humanity's curse-by-ignorance? For tens of thousands of years, we have committed wanton killing–acts that have incrementally denigrated the most overlooked aspect of sophisticated consciousness, in turn diminishing the human-specie's longevity. Each dog killed by humanity, such as by "animal control," is guilty of the blasphemy of needlessly killing an innocent, dysfunctional dog.

How does the academic's argument permit the killing continuance in animal shelters, and by the whims of superficial families?

Does the Rainbow Bridge Exist?

I wonder what hunters who have family dogs think when their dog dies. Do they love and mourn their dog's death? How fraudulent are their tears of grief? Do hunters unknowingly evoke a narrow chasm of sorrow and grief or acquiesce life's fated destiny as cover to still "feel something"? Does their dog's Soul cross the Rainbow Bridge?[61] And if so, how does the reconciliation of this version of grief by the hands that end their lives–the hunter, the veterinarian, the animal control officer, even the so-called dog expert be real? Can their tears, tributes, or whispered regrets avoid feeling contrived when killing has become a sanctioned participation of their practice?

So often, dysfunctional dogs are killed by veterinarians and animal control. What is really being killed is not danger, but consciousness complexity–dysfunctions too nuanced for human patience, too demanding for empathetic growth. Simple dysfunctions too complex, thus retarding humanity's empathetic maturation.

And here's the question that haunts: if Heaven welcomes the hunter's beloved dog and cat, does it not also welcome every other animal the hunter has killed? Will the hunter's personal Rainbow Bridge grow more crowded with each life taken, every deer, bear, or lion waiting alongside their dog?

Does the Rainbow Bridge exist with God?[62]

The utility of familial-species belies irony.

Why Dogs Lick Our Faces

When your dog licks your face, it's not an endearing, heartwarming behavior.

---

[61] https://en.wikipedia.org/wiki/Rainbow_Bridge_(pets)

[62] http://bit.ly/4gQBjSF

Interest and Investigation: Firstly, dogs that lick faces usually do so out of immaturity and underdeveloped emotive structure. The behavior reflects a limited emotive envelope and often stems from a transactional upbringing–one where the individual lacked deep, intimate interactions with humans outside their immediate family group. This leaves the individual insecure about their role in the family group and suppresses their ability to develop true self-awareness and a sophisticated introspective.

Face-licking predicates low self-esteem and low self-worth. It's erroneous to perceive your dog as "always happy" or just that way. Rather, face-licking is a dysfunctional behavior that is extremely detrimental to stabilization and rehabilitation. Face-licking stems from your dog over-exceeding their limited introspective capacity to cogently comprehend their emotive spikes, such as excitement, wildness, or uncouthness. Your dog feels insecure in their familial relationship. This is somewhat akin to the addressable happy-tail.[63] Both can be stabilized in all dogs, regardless of whether they are normal or dysfunctional. What the individual needs is a safe harbor and the ability to idiomatically contextualize their circumstances' immediacy.

When a dog licks a face, their behavior, including licking and body articulation, is overly energetic. This reflects emotional immaturity rather than affection. The licking itself occurs at various speeds, intensities, and body behaviors, which are driven by personality.

Emotionally mature and socially well-adjusted cogent dogs neither face-lick nor display "happy-tail" behaviors. For dysfunctional dogs exhibiting face-licking or happy-tail upon intake, these behaviors will gradually diminish–and eventually cease–through self-realization, a structure of introspection. This requires providing a safe harbor and consistent idiomatic contextualization, transforming encounters with a favored person from a desperate plea for affection into a mutually desired, routine experience. Far too often happy-tail results in unnecessary amputation.

Face-licking is not driven by inherent curiosity or desire to investigate the world through their senses, even though dogs rely on smell and taste to routinely explore the world surrounding them. Instead, the frantic licking of a face, item, or scent is due to greater introvertive interest stemming from your dog's need to obsessively (read: *immaturely*) confirm through direct

[63] http://bit.ly/4glZ4Sg

sampling what they are smelling. This immature, compulsive behavior is a redundancy in their cogent processing and is similar to when a dog smells then licks another dog's urine.

Speaking of the dog that occasionally face-licks, your face is a particularly intriguing canvas. It's an area rich in various scents and tastes. Your skin, your breath, and even the traces of food or other elements will pique their interest when you first come home. Your face becomes a fascinating territory for exploration. They smell and lick both sides of your face to determine distinctness and differentiation, such as where you were traveling by the smell of your face. Excessive face-licking is your dog focusing all of their jagged, excited, immature emotions on you physically with the most articulate part of the body: the tongue. In contrast, a cogently mature and healthily independent dog has confidence in their one-on-one relationship with their human parent and known family or friends.

The Art of Giving Peanut Butter: Decoding Tongue Behavior

Tongue behavior is both contextual and textural, offering a unique perspective into canine cogency. When I gave Nero a large glob of peanut butter, his tongue's response provided evolutionary insights into the subtle nuances dogs interact within their very immediate environment. Comprehension is introvertively idiomatically aggregated.

The immense flexibility and strength of your dog's tongue must be considered, as it performs relentless work for even mundane tasks, such as scooping up water or food. Sharp edges teaches the individual how to physically manipulate items inside their mouth with precision.

When Nero was almost eleven years old, I gave him, along with Sammie and Walter, a large spoonful of peanut butter for a snack in the living room of the rancher. I went to our bedroom, and Nero came to find me for more peanut butter. I deliberately shaped an extra-large round dollop of peanut butter. I realized that tongue behavior wasn't random or involuntary but rather had excellent physical articulation. This level of detailed articulation didn't make sense to exist without functionally significant control.

The manner familial-species lick their faces coincided with various homogeneous circumstances. Licking the left or right side, as well as the front or center, including up to the top of the nose was always done with a controlled measure of length, movement, speed, musculature rigidity, cadence and rhythm, maintained consistently due to deliberacy. It is always circumstance-driven, indicating deliberate physical movement, such as a child sticking their tongue out while trying to figure out a math problem. Crossing left- and right-brain functions in behavior, manifesting physically, makes sense–and the tongue operates in a similar way: it is motivated, not motorized. Similarly, behaving physiologically since the tongue's musculature is so much longer and widely articulable, which indicates such evolutionally complex flexibility was consciousnessly influenced.

When Nero took the large dollop of peanut butter into his mouth, he knew it was peanut butter. The size being much larger surprised Nero. Nero moved the dollop into the back of his mouth, pushing his tongue upward against it to gauge the density. Noting it was soft, Nero immediately released the dollop from the back of his mouth, letting it fall forward towards his lips. The front of his tongue catches it to reassess the consistency and texture, as well as the overall hardness, and to determine how hard to bite if needed to break it apart. Nero pushed the dollop against the front roof of his mouth. Upon discovering it was soft, Nero swallowed it without chewing. Nero assessed in under one second. Texturally, Nero's tongue quickly recognized size, consistency, volume, and mass, as well as malleability, contextually recognizing how it felt in conjunction with taste.

Licking to the left is a cognitive and logical behavior, which extends to the eye and blink behavior, manifesting from analytical processing. The right is anticipatory, cogency manifesting emotional *and* psychological processing.

Eyebrow behaviors are functionally separate. Raising the left eyebrow usually signals: *"I wasn't sure,"* while the right eyebrow conveys, *"I thought so."* These are typically voluntary.

It's also essential to observe *how* tongue behavior manifests: the height of licking, the direction it extends, its speed, and the accompanying movement are all important in comprehending what your dog is cogently processing. Tongue behaviors are quantifiably identifiable across familial-species–lions, cougars, wolves, and hyenas–demonstrating a shared communicative structure.

When dogs lick the front of their mouth and nose, it's a strategic analysis.

- **Shorter, controlled licks to the bottom of their nose** indicate an attempt to consciousnessly balance logical and emotional structures through self-control–a kind of introspective "ego-selfishness", which is similar to human cogency.
- **Quicker, seemingly furtive licks** reflect self-control under greater, heightened emotive demand (not duress nor eustress). Your dog is trying to control and suppress their own emotional and physical agitation. This is not nervousness, but an introvertive indecisiveness. Self-awareness isn't self-preservation, but rather it predicates upon threat assessment and builds a need for self-preservation: *"Should I attack this person? What if I lose?"*–a defensive, introspective driving force, driving flight first, then fight.
- **A straight-up frontal lick** is pensive indecisiveness.
- **A straight-out lick** is the expression of self-aware emotional constraint. The movement appears quick and obtrusively apparent.
- **Higher center licks above the nose** are attempts to recalibrate oneself during heightened emotive circumstances.
- **Higher left licks** convey confirmation ("okay" through to "I thought so").
- **Higher right licks** embody anticipatory emotive introspectiveness.
- **Lower licks** generally indicate cognitive conclusiveness, with subtle variants relative to efficient processing.

Dogs Jump On Us Because...

The behavior of jumping and face-licking are closely related. Jumping is due to strong emotive urgency. Yet there are distinctions: *an excited, jumpy greeting* is different from *a measured, rhythmic jump* that ensures direct contact–more akin to *pawing*. In this sense, jumping is a deliberate control of cogently-thought ***want*** for physical contact and affection.

Dogs, while contextually simple in their social intra-, co-, and interdependencies, display psychological motivations that consciousnessly sustain thoughts. Even when lying down with eyes shut–appearing "asleep"–an evolutionary adaptation for maintaining extreme alertness with eyes shut due to functional sentience for awareness of their surroundings.

For some dogs, jumping up repeatedly is due to above-average intradependency. In these cases, your dog needs to reconcile several layered emotives: affection for you, the sense of abandonment during your absence, and the sustained introspection during the time you were away. These are complex, foreign emotive structures to attempt to decipher cogently. Calm reset-hugs are significantly beneficial in stabilizing and stopping jumping.

To teach your dog that it's not necessary to jump up on you when coming home, you can follow these steps:

1. Calmly enter your home and close the door quietly.
2. Speak in your normal voice–avoid raising your pitch or inflection (VoiceKey1).
3. Please refrain from immediately removing your shoes or jacket. Instead, calmly squat or kneel so you are at your dog's head level.
4. Expect your dog to jump. Center your body to avoid being knocked over accidentally.
5. If your dog jumps at you immediately when you get in the door, use your open hand (fingers together, palm flat) to gently block your dog's forehead. Place the heel of your palm over the center of their forehead–like softly palming a basketball–while being careful not to poke their eyes. Continue gently centering your palm as they move, using a steady, gentle touch and calm voice
6. Give your dog a calm, extended-length reset-hug.

Anxiety and Excitement

Some dogs may jump when they are anxious, excited, or emotionally overwhelmed. Others may dart back and forth, spin in circles, grab a favorite toy and parade it around, bring it to you but not let you take it, or give it to you only to snatch it back. This relates to dysfunctional dogs that exhibit dysfunctional behavior, such as chewing or swallowing items or clothing. This hyper-behavior is a blatant expression of attempting to self-soothe a highly complex emotive structure that isn't foreign to your dog. It's not disobedience or "wildness." Rather, it's your dog's cogent attempt, albeit immature, at self-controlling their emotional excitement–an egocentric awareness that one's emotional complexity is self-addressable, despite seemingly not being self-addressable to their human parent.

Not all expressions of heightened energy should be weighed the same. Anxiety and excitement may look similar on the surface, but they are distinct dysfunctions. Anxiety stems from psychological awareness of one's familial dependencies. The individual's exposure to risks affects physical, emotive structures and psychological safety, which can be both founded and unfounded due to broad influences, whereas excitement predicates upon core default emotives: rage and joy. Excitement is contextualized as joy, offering only a narrow level of cogency–minimal emotional maturation. Excitement provides a purely single-directional cause-and-effect relationship–physical expression to quell introspectively limited emotive processing.

What Does My Dog Think When I Masturbate?

It's crucial to remember that interpreting this action requires a frame of reference. There's no sexual comprehension or predilection interpreted by dogs and animals other than simple observation. Your dog isn't concluding anything remarkable other than seeing you "scratch" yourself. Nor your frequency, speed, or manner of consequence. The subsequent smell is of no great consequence–your dog smells your body's intimate parts often. And though a "higher scent concentration" results from masturbation, it would neither influence nor alarm your dog to conclude anything greater than you've engaged in a prolonged "self-scratch" session.

The concern arising is whether your masturbating behavior is physically or vocally odd. If your physical behavior is frantic or abnormal compared to your dog's familiarity with your normal behavior, your masturbation will cause your dog concern and cognitive confusion (re: threat assessment). If you're vocally loud, contrary to your usual tone, that can exacerbate your dog's concerns about your behavior. There is no functionally common desire by either gender of dogs to consider their sexual interaction (such as humping).

If objects or toys are involved, your dog will likely view them as playthings. To your dog, an item you use might seem like one of their shared play items. If your dog ever sees you using toys while masturbating, they could misinterpret it as an invitation to play or interact with those objects in the future.

It's essential to be aware of your dog's presence and comfort when engaging in any intimate activities. Some dogs may become curious, others will simply ignore it, and some may even become afraid or alarmed at their human surrogate parent behaving in "anger" or "distress." In these cases, your dog might approach to check on you, trying to reconcile their feelings or confusion. Others may be alarmed and interpret you as being unstable or even a potential threat to them.

A dog's perception of their human's masturbation is rooted in their *irrelevance* of superficial sexual gratification and simple associations.

VoiceKey

VoiceKey is the unique tonal musicality of your voice, which your dog finds interesting and captivating. If the family's language is not the same as the local language, maintaining the tone of the local language is important in providing your dog with externally typical societal tones. Nor an emotionally-disingenuous tone. Use the same voice you use in your everyday conversations. This is typically your normal voice with limited intonation, initially monotone.

It's profoundly important to speak your normal, genuine familial voice. Practicing consistency in your verbal communication is critical to utilizing your existing vocal musculature (which becomes critically beneficial in dangerous circumstances). It's common for humans not to communicate earnestly with their dogs. Despite your hope of overt, blatant expressions of communication from your dog, trust your anthropomorphic intuition. **Don't** speak in contrived or disingenuous high-pitched tones. High-pitch elicits play, prey, and predatory interest. The critical influence lies in using sufficient lung volume for breath control to generate a louder sound, thereby avoiding the emotive harshness and pitch that often accompany loud voices.

VoiceKeys range from one to 10. You should self-scale so that VoiceKey1 is your "normal voice" and VoiceKey10 is "screaming, emotionally loud," which is used for extreme circumstances, such as (breaking up vicious) fighting. Start always from VoiceKey1. Your typical day ranges up to VoiceKey4 (loud voice). Raising your voice emotionally also creates emotive or tonal harshness, which can be disturbing and has the detriment of becoming known as your "normal" voice. In turn, this pushes your VoiceKey range higher and higher. VoiceKey1 should always be your typical vocal day. In one example, (the third video in the playlist[64]), after finally getting Mingki into my car, I begin quickly testing and determining which tones Mingki understood best.

The Role of VoiceKey and Touch

Both co-relate and can intra-relate, as both are evolved forms of bi-communication. Touch and VoiceKey entail reciprocal interaction: "a compassionate person touches you." Both require self-awareness, thereby fostering sophisticated introspection to construct your dog's ego, enhancing the desire to comprehend egocentrically, and maturing the objectification of self and others. To have deliberate, elective interest in your touch and voice at a significant level of intimacy and trust–especially for dogs that are dysfunctional or abused–communication and interactions of any form must always be from their perspective.

The human-dog analogy is similar to the movie *Forrest Gump*. Toward the end of the movie, there's a scene where Tom Hanks' character, Forrest Gump, is standing at the bottom of the stairs looking up at the love of his life, Jenny. Forrest looks at her and says, "I'm not a smart man, but I know what love is." We see Forrest's visceral sincerity in his love for Jenny. *True love.* Like the white picket fence or Romeo and Juliet's "I'd die for you" kind of indomitable love. We understand Forrest's profound, genuine love entirely. We feel within our bodies the love Forrest holds for Jenny. We understand and comprehend exactly how Forrest feels.

In the movie, Forrest is established as having an IQ of 78 and is often called "retarded." How could Forrest even understand real love, modern-day love? The kind where there's love, joy, sadness, jealousy, anger, abandonment, elation, and fears, as well as the mundane: bills to pay, work to do, goals to achieve, vacations to share, etc. Forrest can't understand *true love* at *our* complex, modern, and sophisticated level. Yet we totally understand Forrest's level of love, which is less sophisticated in emotive construction relative to his structure of consciousness.

We recognize the way Forrest talks to Jenny (VoiceKey), how he listens to her, and how he longs for her touch. When Forrest does hold Jenny's hand, he isn't extravagantly infatuated nor excitedly hyper or elated when they're

---

64 Arf Arf Bark Bark Rescue & Rehab, "Mingki From Animal Hope and Wellness Foundation playlist," *YouTube,* https://www.youtube.com/playlist?list=PLK43vpl6h3zZHdeWx-KPdes5gKdXaf6CM

physically affectionate and endearing. Forrest and Jenny are content and enjoying the quiet and calmness of the affection. There are no fidgeting mannerisms, childish elative behavior, or petting or rubbing the person they love. Forrest remains still and motionless from trust, not nervousness. Stillness in touch and voice are crucially important and are key parts of "step one" for any trusting relationship. In contrast, *motion* can evoke nervousness, insecurities, unreliability, and disingenuity, undermining familial safety, much like a trembling voice or a shaking knee.

When you meet someone with clearly identifiable cognitive issues, you don't "talk down to the person." Instead, you use language adjusted to what you believe is within the individual's comprehension capacity. You gauge their comprehension through their verbal and physical responses or psychosomatic manifestations. You adjust your speed of talking and lessen extraneous hand and body movements (this is homogeneous in the human-specie). You adjust your interactions to accommodate their cognitive dysfunction. You touch them reciprocally to their body behavior. You employ your field-of-vision processing, empathy, objectification, and introspection structures as critical analyses of the cognitive person.

For dogs to comprehend being touched (hypersensitivity, flinch response, the intimacy of affection) predicates upon sophisticated emotive construction to process and discern where the physical contact falls on the scale–pleasure, discomfort, pain, or injury–who is touching them (trust, familiarity). Stillness of touch is highly critical in providing consistent reliability with VoiceKey.

Touch must always be smooth, consistent, and once in contact, motionless while physically connected. Quick hand movements, such as petting or "soothing rubs," don't benefit your dysfunctional dog; instead, they reflect human nervousness. Such movements are distracting and convey un-security and insecurity (similar to nervous knee-shaking).

To manage these dynamics effectively, it's crucial to use touch with slow, predictable body-behavior movement flow. Use the "same approach" every time during the initial weeks or months to rehabilitate traumas and stabilize ancillary/consequential dysfunctions. Some dogs may not be accustomed to being touched in certain areas of their body due to prior abuse, so compassion and caution must be used judiciously.

The benefit of using VoiceKey (with and without physical contact) is that your VoiceKey1 has an established neutral tone and sound. This allows you to adopt a simple protocol approach of being consistent and predictable in your voice and behavior by always starting your voice neutrally– "step one"–every time you interact. You teach your dog that you're emotionally, physically, and vocally predictable.

Abused dogs' histories are typically due to abuse or neglect, which reflects "unpredictable human-specie behavior," causing them to emotionally and urgently defend themselves from perceived danger from unusual human behavior (a causal cyclic reciprocated trauma). Using VoiceKey1 allows for greater opportunity for common familiarity, which interests your dog in paying attention to any nuances of your voice (key) in different contexts and circumstances. This encourages sophisticated cogency, self-actualization, self-soothing, and healthy intradependency.

This helps immensely during negative circumstances or interactions, so they hear you in VoiceKey1 to vocally provide a safe harbor and idiomatically contextualize their circumstance for historical comparison. This allows you to create a VoiceKey range of interaction to graduate the individual's context for self-actualization and self-soothing.

I give frequent physical contact through reset-hugs and the stillness of physical touch with my hand. I would keep my hand flat-palmed and motionless against my dog's body during the initial seven to twelve seconds of physical connection. I would calmly say phrases "(name), you're okay," "you're okay (name)," "(name) come here," or "(name) give me a hug." Caution is advised, as there are specific emotional structures of comprehension that your dog will consider when you switch the order of their name. When giving reset-hugs or physical touch to contextualize my presence for inclusive familial protection and parental safety–particularly in circumstances where your dog may perceive grave potential threats–I may simultaneously talk *with* them using VoiceKey1 to prudently reassure them calmly.

This is done using a narrow envelope of emotive or tonal voice, spoken with a regular volume of breath–the calmness of a parent.

By motionlessly touching and vocally reassuring them, you familiarize yourself with the individuality of your dog in real time, proving that you are there with them when they feel most vulnerable (abandonment dysfunction). You are your dog's human surrogate parent. Your dog can trust you to parentally defend them because you are proving so by being physically at their side and "holding their hand" calmly (it's not "your dog is protecting you"). You are willing to physically protect your dog with your own body. This is intrinsically familial.

Keeping in mind the context of symmetry of being touched on one side of their body isn't equally or automatically applicable to your dog with their "other side." A complementary reset-hug for your dog's opposite side will comprehensively confirm their self-awareness of their body's sameness, the "other side." This provides physical self-objectification, along with the visceral evolution of your dog's empathetic structure of self. "Hug Stephen's left side."

Understanding these interactions, which are 100 percent effective with all dogs, sheds light on complex social dynamics in a manner and perspective that recognizes the shared species' familialism and emotional isomorphic evolution. Your dog's reliance on you is as great as, and the same as that of a child on its parent, and you are their greatest protector from hunger and harm. It's an opportunity to maintain and sustain the bonds you share with each furry Soul that has blessed your lifetime. It flows within a familially harmonious and secure environment for everyone.

IMPORTANT: You must speak very short sentences (two to five words) **in contiguous format, normal tone, and cadence as sentences spelled WITHOUT spaces**: **"Neroyou'reokay" and "Waltercomehere" so that you are speaking one long word (not recitative).** "(Name)you'reokay," "(name) givemeahug," "(name)comehere."

The Soul of a Dog Reset-Hug: How to Use It?

1. With your dog's body perpendicular to yours, stand facing your dog's mid-torso with their head on your left side and their bum on your right side. It will look as if you're standing facing your dog's rib cage with your knees. You can start or switch between the right and left sides.

2. If your dog is smaller, squat down to their height. Be careful not to lose your balance and accidentally fall back or forward at any time. You must be physically stable. This is the founding basics of "step one." You must not cheat in this exercise by leaning over your dog, placing your hand or arm on their back, or applying any downward weight on them. If your dog is larger, you would need to squat

slightly without leaning to be able to perform the reset-hug skillfully. Don't be physically off-center when reset-hugging by maintaining your body mechanics.

3. Now that you're squatting and your dog is perpendicular to you, gently place their throat in the inside crook of your left arm. Your left hand's open palm will be raised to lightly hold the right side of your dog's face and head—an embrace.

4. With your right arm, bring it up and over the top of your dog's back and right side, then downward along the outside of their body's right side. Continue moving your right arm until you're lightly wrapping your right hand slightly to the left of your dog's front legs, under the left side of their chest. This will resemble a full-body, football-style hug.

5. Using the fingers or palm of your right hand, move it until you can feel your dog's heartbeat. This can be done with all sizes of dogs, including Chihuahuas. Now, you can gauge your dog's heart rhythm and pattern (such as checking for irregular patterns for heart murmurs). You'll often feel the pace of your dog's heartbeat physiologically change pattern from fast to slower.

6. You can feel your dog's respiratory pattern.

7. You can sense your dog's body and how they are physically structured. Is your dog standing relaxed, semi-rigid, or tensely? This is your dog's "*physical gait structure,*" whether they're significantly, physically tense, seeming restless, or leaning into or away from you.

8. Study your dog's four-paw position stance. Are all four paws in a normal symmetrical pattern? Is one paw on your foot or very close to it? Are your dog's back paws symmetrical, but their front paws are staggered or narrow/wide apart? Analogy: we observe how someone stands, noting their foot position and how it affects their physical structure. Psychosomatically, your dog will stand in a manner that directly reflects how they feel and what they're thinking. This has been crucial for my work.

9. With your dog's throat still in the crook of your inside elbow, you can feel if they're turning their head away or to you. You can feel if they're

looking around just by their physical behavior. If this happens, look in the same direction your dog is looking and calmly say, in that direction, "(name)you'reokay."

10. Never place any weight onto your hands on your dog's back, especially when you're standing up. This often happens when people are trying to stand up. If they lose balance even slightly, they may inadvertently use their dog's back to steady their rise. However, they often end up pushing or placing the weight of their hands down onto their dog's back, which creates confusion and unnecessarily causes psychological disruption. It can also potentially damage your dog's back, as dogs lack the musculature integrity to bear weight (which is why weighted-dog backpacks and sled/weight pulling are detrimental to your dog's long-term physical health).

11. Reset-hugs can be given at any time, not just when your dog needs protection and stabilization. Random reset-hugs are a great way to revisit the familial relationship with your beloved dog, akin to your romantic partner sending you a mid-day text saying, *"I'm thinking of you."* Random reset-hugs throughout the day also allow you to continuously practice intuitive gauging of your dog's physical and emotional structure.

    By reconciling your intuition about your dog through reset-hugs, you teach yourself to further understand your dog's behavior, learning more nuanced aspects with each reset-hug. You're aggregating all structures of your dog's daily emotives by mentally mapping your dog's idiomatic contextualization succinctly onward with each reset-hug.

12. Please always remember that if your dog is dysfunctional, they will not be accustomed to receiving reset-hugs and may likely express emotional concerns about intimacy of affection. Don't do anything that may cause you or anybody injury or damage to property.

13. From birth to juniorhood, physical affection is largely predicated upon the type and strength of emotional health conveyed through familial protection and upbringing, as well as healthy structures of intra- and inter-dependencies. These flow into the structures of egocentrism and egoselfishness, which are used to construct

empathy and objectification of self and others. This is clearly crucial in human development due to our sophisticated consciousness.

In dogs, this is miscomprehended as the "two fear periods." Similar to the oft bandied statements, "I guess her dad didn't love her enough when she was a child" or "he doesn't care if he gets good or bad attention as long as he gets attention", such miscomprehensions label a person "alpha" or "A-type" personality. We intrinsically know the brash person is seeking (any kind of) attention due to psychological insecurity (i.e., school bullies). Yet we materialistically attribute their dysfunctions as an aberrant representation of "alpha" personality. We intuitively know "alpha" people aren't actually alpha and domineering, but rather individuals with low self-esteem who psychosomatically manifest profound indecisiveness or insecurity. The traditional label marginalizes the root causation. The person roots their dysfunctions in deficient self-esteem, self-worth, and self-confidence, as well as either low or high intradependency.

Dogs will attack because they feel afraid, unprotected, and alone—without protection from "family." This is not the grossness of genericisms of "aggressive" and "fearful" that cause any dog to attack; but rather to a dog's genuine fear of being attacked or provoked first. It follows the logic of flight, *then* fight. A solid reset-hug for between twelve to seventeen seconds is ideal during initial rehabilitation (everyone's safety is always in mind). This allows your dog to feel the rehabilitating physical affection from your reset-hug viscerally—safe harbor.

14. When I'm working with a predatory dog, I don't focus on eye contact or excessive or complex talking (your behavior is primarily nonverbal and limited in versatility). The reset-hug exercised with a very simple approach. I teach dog parents to focus on watching their beloved dysfunctional dog's whole body and never worry about making eye contact.

15. Both children and domesticated dogs are emotionally mature based on their sense of safety and familial protection: the protection they receive from their family. For example, a newborn puppy curls up against their mother and siblings for warmth and security. In domesticated environments, a newborn puppy is often physically carried and coddled by their human parent. As they grow older and

bigger, they become too heavy or too wiggly to carry or hold, so the same level of intimate affection tends to stop very suddenly. Your dog's level of emotional intradependency gets impacted, which is affective introspectively.

This dysfunction is why the label "fear periods" is missing a fundamental understanding that there's immaturity of emotive processing. The sudden loss of physical affection at such a level of intimate intradepedency from human parents will cause dysfunctions and likewise cause a human child to develop abandonment dysfunction.

For the wild dog, development is very limited and jagged in their emotive and introspective nature. In contrast, wild wolves, tigers, and horses have been socially habilitated into a domestic context. This essentially means that randomly born familial-species have the corresponding ability to adjust their rudimentary emotional and logical processes cogently, thereby developing their sophisticated capacity to comprehend living with a different apex specie indoors. This is literally the same as a "space alien abducting you as their personal companion."[65] The functional comprehension to adapt wholesale to a disingenuous environmental context, such as living indoors, is fundamental to the cogency of consciousness and reflects the functions of self-objectification, objectification, and introspection, which construct empathetic processing–emotive isomorphism.

16. Reset-hugs carry that sense of safety from infancy, when a child naturally expects the constant physical, emotional, and psychological protection from their parents. These are contextualized in relation to the foundational robustness of emotional health and, of course, the ongoing conflationary aggregation of circumstances that are both emotionally and demonstrably similar (such as abandonment). Foundating structures that are idiomatic-referencing of familial and intradependency are mnemonical for "memories," and conflation can begin contexting into abandonment, which produces a feeling of being unprotected. Other than the sudden reduction of being carried, nothing else in the home has identifiably changed–akin to two people madly in love with each other for years, but then over

[65] https://en.wikipedia.org/wiki/A_Man_Called_Horse_(film)

time, one of them begins to feel their partner doesn't love them equally.

Reset-hugs allow for the development of emotive and physical memories into a recallable historical context (like reminiscing about the safety of puppyhood). Much like the feeling of receiving a hug from a good friend you haven't seen in years, these hugs allow you to emotively process your emotional and psychological latencies that surface anew.

17. Aside from your dysfunctional dog standing or leaning against you, it's illogical to assume the carrying and coddling of puppyhood are forever lost in the adult dog due to "innate predation predominance." Whether we're talking about Lincoln, Nero, Hugo,[66] or a "normal, happy dog," behavior is psychologically homogenous–and predation is simple to rehabilitate.

    Think of it this way: if an unknown stranger on the street suddenly walked up and gave you a hug, you'd recoil. But if an old friend wrapped you in an embrace after years apart, you'd welcome it with warmth. There's a visceral feeling. And if it's a friend you hug frequently, those hugs become somewhat practiced and distant from the visceral hug of a long-lost friend.

    In the same way, teaching a predatory and dysfunctional dog to once again accept physical affection requires sincerity. Every interaction–physical or verbal–must be genuine. Consistency matters, or at the very least, predictability. Trustworthiness is foundational.

18. These manners of physical and verbal context, in various circumstances, are fundamentally predicated emotional-processing structures that consciousnessly gauge and recall comparisons of similar or identical circumstances in aggregate conflation. Reset-hugs provide tempering of such visceral familiarity, serving as a foundational base for rebuilding a dysfunctional dog's self-esteem, self-worth, and self-confidence while demonstrating parental affection and protection as when carried during puppyhood.

[66] http://bit.ly/3loUq9G

19. Contrary to the saying, "not all dogs love hugs." Familial-species lack germane familiarity beyond infancy and juvenile stages, yet are inherently fond of affection. For instance, consider the hand-holding analogy: your dog learns to feel comfortable with their complex foreign emotions relative to their ego-centric structure due to the degree of intimacy of physical affection. This is imperative for processing the complexity of affection.

    Hugs are an extremely intimate, shared physical interaction that requires profound trust. It requires significant risk to be exposed to another apex specie: human. To learn to seek and trust that my physicality is trustworthy and protective by placing their need for familial protection first. Applying reset-hugs during significantly heightened, confrontation and emotional circumstances–such as seeing or encountering another dog in on-leash and off-leash situations, including dog parks–is psychologically beneficial for the extremely dysfunctional dogs that I rehabilitate.

    Some dogs may manifest negative behavior towards being hugged due to prior emotional traumas that cause intimacy-of-affection dysfunction, including unfamiliarity, insincerity, and a lack of consistency. Understanding your dog's behaviors is more akin to Forrest Gump in real life, with equitable respect for his comprehension. You watch Forrest's physical movements for signs of comprehension or lack of. You adjust your words, including your tone of voice and pattern. This is structurally similar to how English as a Second Language (ESL) students are taught the English language. This is crucial to maturing how your dog learns to process their complex emotions. I apply reset-hugs during times of complex emotive processing. At first, it's extremely risky, but with patient consistency over days and weeks, I am able to calm potentially perilous and extremely dangerous circumstances with reset-hugging.

20. Reset-hugs for both the right and left sides of your dog are encouraged (if time allows). This provides greater dimensional-self comprehension; both are equally registrable within your dog's comprehension. Keeping in context the left and right brain processing that conflates actual physical contact during heightened emotional circumstances. Your dog psychologically perceives egocentrically. I typically give one-sided reset-hugs due to my limited time. If there's danger, the reset-hug will be on my dog's side, where my backside

physically faces toward my dog's perceived threat–proving that I'm willing to protect "us" with my life, which is a trait that predates early puppyhood in the wild and domestication. I empirically demonstrate familial protection through the reset-hug, which teaches my dogs that they don't need to protect "us." Not "me." We're both familial-species, hence a corresponding dilutive scale of cogency and emotive processing in the child-parent dependency structure.

21. It's essential to protect your dog from perceived dangers, such as people, dogs, baby-strollers, vehicles, while on a walk. If your dog becomes scared, place your body between them and the perceived danger. Applying reset-hugs optimally as soon as your dog recognizes the danger, not you. Your dog may start to freeze up, wildly wander on a leash, and frequently look at you. **Don't** wait or delay the reset-hug because your dog's significant processing speed allows emotions to be expressed quickly. I make sure my center of gravity and body mechanics aren't going to cause me to topple over.

22. While applying a reset-hug, I always say phrases such as: "(name) you'reokay," "Hisillyboy" / "Hisillygirl," "(name)comehere," or "(name) givemeahug" **in contiguous format, normal tone, and cadence. Almost as if pronouncing a diphthong or triphthong.** These phrases further contextualize the definitions of existing known "words." Evolving cogency. These provide emotive breadth in developing emotional-psychological idiomatic contextualization of known words–visceral maturity. As language developed via emotive contextualization, self-awareness develops through reset-hugs, which are familially protective and emotionally embracing and consoling. This supports healthy intradependency.

Behaviorism Beyond Dogs: Exploring Consciousness in All Animals

Behavior is homogeneously congruently recognizable in familial-species. The realm of behaviorism extends far. It encompasses all creatures, from the familiar to the extraordinary, such as Kaluha the Alpaca[67]. The human-specie's

[67] Tsai, James. "Kaluha the Alpaca," December 6, 2017. https://www.facebook.com/TheSoulOfaDog/posts/10159650884030402.

quest to understand behavior and consciousness in animals presents us with fascinating opportunities for exploration.

Kaluha and James

It's a step toward unlocking the mysteries of consciousness in all creatures. Kaluha is a remarkable individual with his unique dysfunctions: his need for acknowledgment and a desire to escape loneliness. Kaluha's behaviors, responses, and interactions with the world around him provide valuable insights into consciousnesses, reproofing my theorem. I absolutely expected my theorem to be equally correct and effective, and I was 100 percent correct. I envision a future academia that comprehends consciousness dilutively in a wide array of familial-species, with *The Soul of a Dog* addressing miscomprehensions. It's a journey of discovery that holds the potential to deepen our understanding of the rich tapestry of consciousness.

CHAPTER 14

Theorem of Consciousness and of Learning

Biological Consciousness in Dogs, Animals, and Humans

In the quest to unravel the enigmatic nature of consciousness, Temple University, a prestigious institution, embarked on a competition aimed at elucidating why and how we experience feelings. The overarching question at the center of this is, "What is consciousness?" In this exploration, I will endeavor to present a simple yet compelling theorem of consciousness and of learning that resonates intuitively.

Does human consciousness seem perhaps the most remarkable biological feat on Earth, and potentially remarkably competitive with other evolved consciousnesses in the universe? Is it a mere chance that we, as an Earth autochthonous specie, have achieved self-awareness and, crucially, the ability to be objectively self-aware of others empathetically?

Temple University errs by asking lineal questions, expecting logical epiphanies. How do we discern emotions and perceptions? Does consciousness underpin memories, or is it a byproduct of our continual stream of life experiences–a premeditated abstraction of time and egocentric perspectives rooted in linear thinking? Attribute consciousness to a random biological byproduct, or do memories represent the cumulative outcome of a series of biological compartmentalizations stored in our brains for historical reference? Is there a correlation with Darwinism? Why does consciousness remain one of the most elusive challenges in science, pushing the brightest minds to postulate and even posit wildly ridiculous theories?

Why do consciousness theorists sidestep the basic principles of logical mathematic biology? Agreed evolutionary theory serves as a foundational premise for formulating a thorough understanding of consciousness and its biological practicality.

One easily accessible specie that's functionally "consciousness" resides under our very noses–dogs. The ability of dogs to differentiate between the comfort of a soft, warm dog bed and the discomfort of a hard floor showcases consciousness as functionally introspective and egocentric.

Consciousness is rooted solely in evolutionary biology. When working with extremely dysfunctional dogs, recognizing behaviors indicative of sentience is paramount. Severe behavioral issues such as mauling humans or killing other dogs are analogous to human psychosis behaviors. Disaggregating and destructuring are the correct protocols to accurately upstream the cause of the dysfunction that initiates the problem. Phylogenesis always begins with a minor emotional infraction relative to familial dependencies. Recognizing sentience is equivalent to recognizing equitable behavior, a.k.a. quantification of consciousness. Consciousness exists with sophisticated cogency; self-awareness and empathetic comprehension shape born predatory conduct, adapting to complex relationships such as cross-species cohabitation and domestication consciousnessly. Your dog's comfort, security, and codependence mirror human desires.

Consciousness fundamentally evolves around the self and the imperative to avoid emotional, psychological, and physical pains. This survival mechanism requires a strong sense of self to initiate immediate responses to potential threats and enduring fears. In contrast, logic operates independently of the self because cognition is linear. This duality reflects our evolutionary journey, stemming from an era when the human-specie evolved into its survival strategies through self-awareness, evolving toward deliberate cohesive collaborations with other individuals within a structured societal framework.

Consciousness, at its core, represents an ego-driven endeavor for survival borne out of each familial-specie's sophisticated interpretation of communal unison, not the ability to talk, but not to feel alone and unprotected. We understand death because we process emotional pain internally along with endurement. Dogs, also a familial-specie, experience the loss[68] or disappearance of loved ones. Death introduces highly complex emotional experiences that most humans don't outwardly manifest, either. You would rarely know if your coworker's family had died unless you were informed.

[68] http://bit.ly/46lGKUP

An individual's unique behavior reflects natural emotional variances beyond specie-stereotypic behavior. Psychological dysfunction is always circumstantial, affecting dogs and humans similarly. Disaggregating consciousness necessitates destructuring psychosomatic manifestations so as to comprehend the emotional cause of dysfunction. To ascertain answers, identifying sentient trait markers, in all its complexity, is deeply entwined with emotions.

The examination of consciousness has long been a subject of profound intrigue and debate, with various theories attempting to decode this enigmatic aspect as exclusively human existence. The study of consciousness frequently unfolds within a linear framework, even when exploring the mysteries of quantum mechanics. Imagine consciousness as the faint hum of an enormous factory machine composed of countless production subroutines.

Sentience and the Default of Defense

For sentient beings, defense is always the default mode. To navigate the intricacies of existence, the individual must constantly decide between seeking sustenance and refuge, avoiding threats, and confronting threats. Consider a dog faced with daily beatings. The individual dog is faced with the option of defending themself or accepting the situation. There is no predicate of aggression or offense mounted without the need to protect oneself, which is a defensiveness-predilection. *Flight, then fight* logic guides every individual towards self-protection—a consciousness choice made through introspective awareness to ensure their own well-being. There can be no exercise of offense ("fight") without cause or reason for defensiveness.

Theorem of Consciousness and of Learning

Repeated research correlates that familial-species share similar construction of brains. Complex-to-sophisticated familial-species share similar mapped biological construction structures in the brains, which permits the abstraction of consciousness at a corresponding dilutive scale relative to human sophisticated consciousness; therefore, no demarcation of consciousness exists. This applies to dogs, humans, and familial-species with complex to sophisticated consciousnesses. Both endothermic and exothermic species rely upon this unavoidable default of evolution. This involves looking at the forest *and* the trees simultaneously. Hence, consciousness is fully functional and sophisticated within each specie.

> *Consciousness is the biological compartmentalization of the falsepositive.*

As many people in and out of academia feel and even believe that the construct of consciousness is comprised of complexities, modalities, planes of spirituality, co-functioning/intra-autonomic, extra-dimensional, or divine deliberacy, none of these establish a biological logical sensibility. The biological function of consciousness processes occurs at a corresponding dilutive scale relative to all species, with the human-specie serving self-indulgently as Earth's benchmark. The various postulates and opines on the complexities of consciousness stem from the human-specie's insecure belief that it thinks sophisticated consciousness is biologically exclusive, conceitedly forgetting that the mathematical exactness of evolution, which drives wholesale phylogenetic variation, is a default.

The dozens of centuries of the human-specie's academic geniuses and theorists/philosophers spun their wheels directly because of political ignorance or religious miscomprehension. Failing to comprehend consciousness construction continues to cause literally trillions of animals to suffer under the yoke of utility, servitude, sport, hunting, and food, which certainly offends and contravenes the normal development of the universe.

Consciousness evolution possesses biological mathematical malleability to compartmentalize all learned information; positive, negative, and falsepositive. Biology aggregates, conflates, and stores **all** the answers between "yes and no," "black and white," and "1 and 0." Biological consciousness has the ability to physically store all the finitely-infinite falsepositive "answers", mathematically hereditating consciousness. Evolution compartmentalizes these infinitesimal irrationalities, a.k.a. biological falsepositives whose results populate infinitely in their decimal expansion.

$$C = (<1 \text{ and } >0)$$

Life existed iteratively, pre-Darwin, before Darwinism's stochastic generational evolution. Individualistically, each specie evolved iteratively. Each iterative learned "answers" (physiological and psychosomatic "exhaust manifolding") as a disaggregate: separate lives, at different stages of age, upon a fragile, limited population. Each specie's iterative consciousness construction evolved through aggregating nearly homogeneous, prominent traits via random stochastic popularity. Biology, by default, conflates falsepositives into physical compartmentalization neuronically–"traits" that aggregate into the gradual conflating of evolution of consciousness. This process occurs gossamer-thin: iterative by iterative, layer upon layer, with subtle self-similarity and variegation, mathematically compartmentalizing false positives along a progenic evolutionary mapping gradient.

Through this layering, the sophistication of circumstance, learning and experience evolves into a consecutiveship of biology—a structure capable of emotive processing followed by the construction of memory. Over time, these structures accumulate large-scale volume of "answers," compartmentalized neural biologic by physical electrification (frequency), conflating relevant historical comparatives in real time.

Irrational numbers, such as Pi, whose non-terminating decimal representation ("subdecimal-infinity") expands infinitely beyond physical practicality. Yet, the length of a subdecimal number is infinite; therefore, all subdecimal numbers are of the same length and can be logically computed, albeit abstractive.

If the universe were composed entirely as physical memory, a subdecimal-infinity number would instantly occupy and exceed storage. Many might be dismayed, realizing that human brains are simple, classical computational systems. Irrational mathematic supports biological mathematical malleability, allowing for the hereditas validation of falsepositives within the physical dimension of brains.

To the dismay of academia, which views sophisticated consciousness as human-exclusive, the fact is that "consciousness" exists as randomly as within all species. Demarcating consciousness is the primary reason academia continues to erroneously postulate "human consciousness" as if it were possibly deity-deliberate, intra-autonomic modality, sequence, or a quantum phenomenon. Or if some unique evolutionary biological tweak had deliberately advanced the human-specie's consciousness but cynically withheld from all other species. These opines betray agreed Darwinism and ignore biological mathematic logic. Consciousness foundates all scales relative to the evolutionally engineered schematic from Earth's *"first cells."* Not extravagant uniqueness.

To evolve multiple consciousnesses within the same tenuous ecosystem is not only counter-evolutionary and resource-intensive—it would succumb to Darwinism long before sophisticated biological life began.

Consciousness isn't "fantastical," yet many regarded people postulate thusly. I suspect this is to maintain anthropomorphic demarcation and to intrinsically protect the human-specie's systemic insecurity from the irrefutable biological truth of "not special" existence. Not being a unique existence is what the human-specie cannot fathom nor admit to existential redundancy. Being one of billions of species throughout evolution means accepting that the human-specie is simply a fortunate outcome of random evolution since life varied from *first cells*.

The phylogenesis of consciousness is clearly expected to exhibit homogeneous inherency through evolution. Constructing complex-/sophisticated-consciousnesses required reconciliatory evolution from a "blob of cells" to a diversity of complex biological structures. Causing species with deliberative sentient functioning. Consciousness is further complexed by evolution into empathetic sentience, comprising psychosomatic manifestations. Notwithstanding *static evolution* and *stagnant evolution* eras affective and imperative for most evolving species.

Consciousness, albeit intrinsic and inherent, is constructed into the biological structure as a reconciliatory and default self-check. Consciousness shall occur on any planet whose ecology supports evolution. Foreign planet aliens will mathematically evolve a similar scale of consciousness complexity, other than in terms of degree of intelligence, sophistication of idiomatic contextualization, and empathetic sophistication.

Consciousness, if postulated as subjective by academe, inexplicably then demands all other species to equitably provide identifiable anthropomorphic machinations of sentience via blatant, overt, or obtuse communicable expressions. Despite being a completely disingenuous and one-sided communication or interpretation, this is typically academically anthropomorphized as inconclusive or indeterminable. Individualistic consciousness operates independently within present circumstances, aggregating and conflating with historical comparatives to inform idiomatic contextualization.

Consciousness being introvertively egocentric, with introspective egoselfishness for objectification and self-objectification constructs for an empathetic structure. Empathetic comprehension of self/others/inanimate predicate sophisticated consciousness. The evolution of consciousness is measured through a corresponding dilutive scale, which enables the quantitative identification of behavior. Regardless of stochastic factors, to predicate predictable psychological behavior ranging from comprehending rudimentary logic and emotional processing structures to deliberate psychosomatic manifestations across all species as quantifiable.

Intrinsically present, yet there's no ecological need for familial-species in the wild to require complex memory nor idiomatically contextualize one's social and familial construct beyond immediacy. Complex, fantastical ideations, such as planning and scheduling–setting your alarm clock for work or planning your education or career five years from now–are interspersed among "daily life" and reflect the materialist-predatory nature of the human-specie. Abstracting such complexity is relative to the need, utility, and elicitation of traits in any individual and their emotive-isomorphic sophistication, cognizant of societal habits. Individuals with anomalous and unique higher cogency populate within all species and are often anecdotally noted in broad swaths of familial-species beyond cats, horses, and humans. Sophisticated-consciousness flows within real life improvisationally; hence, empathetic complexity reconciles and evolutionarily spurs introvertive and introspective structures, notwithstanding the statistical randomness of the specie's evolution.

A prime example of sophisticated-consciousness exists in the most commonly domesticated species: cats and dogs. Dogs are emotively prolific in human regions–the sophisticated consciousness to cohabitate with other apex species, especially in domesticated settings that are wholesale disingenuous to all nonhuman familial-species. Comprehending a familial-inclusive psychological context requires significant cogency, coupled with salience, to emotively value and appreciate the disingenuous co- and intra-dependency within cross-species families.

Dogs are born predators, as is the human-specie; hence, the detriment of academically uncouth miscomprehension that dogs lack sophisticated-consciousness, which is why *behavioral euthanasia* is relied upon by the inept. Using *behavioral euthanasia* as an actual "remedy" for dysfunctional, psychologically distressed behavior is truly the most egregious of academic malpractice, reflecting a miscomprehension of consciousness entirely.

Consciousness functions as a physical exhaust manifold through psychosomatic manifestations, essentially in a reliable volumetric response to historical and biological context, which is reconciled iteratively and hereditated through evolution. Each individual/iterative of their specie is uniquely contextual in their brain's overall mapped electrical signature, just as each flake of snow retains its design-individuality regardless of being in a snowstorm or compacted within an iceberg.

Neurotubule natch conducive for boolean consciousness

The frequency and volume of electrical flow through neurotubules seemingly contrast with the theorem's position of frequency as comprised of single iteratives. Frequency flows through neurotubules despite being disaggregate, each journeying as an individual's consciousness.

Within highly intimate and discrete biologic, it's forgivable to think that "quantum consciousness" exists within the wetness. "Quantum consciousness" would demand significant resources, forcing evolution to constructively over-robust the brain—lowering the human-specie's age median averages for brain diseases, lower brain life expectancy, sharper-edged emotions, abrupt cognitive processing, and greater predation. Functionally conflicting against lower-resource organs/physiologic causing input/output interneuronic incongruence; dual-processing as being both quantum and boolean consciousness as evolutionally inefficient, thus attrition through evolution.

Volumic activity in the brain is not a continuous line of electrical frequency but rather single iterations behaving massively in a contiguous manner (very crudely, a starling murmuration-like connectome[69] snowstorm). Biology, evolutionarily and defaultively, allows falsepositives (variants) to be improvisationally exercised and the "results" to be compartmentalized due to neuronic biological mathematical malleability due to the accommodation of decimal expansion's subdecimal infinity (of which information is serially compartmentalized). Neurons spherically exhibit up to 360-degree dendrite manifestation, which permits "nonlinearity" whilst faithfully boolean; the physical construction to compartmentalize falsepositive output. High-use common paths further robust those neurons due to the electrical frequencies that callus the biological neuronal paths, affirming the adage "use it or lose it," as noted in brain health and synaptic pruning. Miniscule biological irritation results from the electrical frequency, causing callusing of neurotubules. Crudely: rope burn that "clears out the roadmap."

---

[69] https://en.wikipedia.org/wiki/Connectome

Electrical bonds, albeit at millivolts, are powerfully equivalent to 500,000 volts. Single-iterative physical journeying intimately proximate or parallel to each other through common neural dendrite paths furthers greater biological callus robustness. There is a higher probability for unnatural electrical "shorting" between higher-use paths, creating unnatural, random connections which contribute to illogic within consciousness. The mathematical irrationality of falsepositives is biologically existent, arising from the creation of new dendrite paths predicated upon improvisation, specifically due to frequency and electrical short-circuiting. Electrically "jumping" from one neuronic pathway into another preexisting neuronic pathway: journeying in a similar direction for part or all of the same distance. "Cutting in line" which creates a new neural pathway biologically strengthened by the electrical callusing. This is an emotional variant within emotive construct–evolution unto sophisticated irrationality: imperatively constructional for consciousness. This provides insight to the physical causation of dementia structures such as Alzheimer's which affect the logic structure of their biological context map of neuronic pattern.

Larger-scale neuronal structures utilize callused "neuronic highways"; they conflate even larger psychological structures, such as traits that evolve fuller emotional breadth in tandem with logic processing. A single-iterative's electrical journey is not a standalone reconciliatory, it is always to a "dead-end" default. Neuronic highways aren't "single-iteratives traveling the same highways altogether" but literally individually-mandated. Single-iterative autonomic travel within collective direction within the "snowstorm." Crystallining reconciles the entire brain at birth for affirming wholesale electrical mapping for frequency harmonization–the uniformity of electrical-bonding forces coursing through neurons, which then requires healing via sleep. Dreaming provides a quasi-consciousness state where only key sustaining neural systems throughout (neo: "neuronicality") are reconciled. This is akin to leaving a few lights on in an office building overnight.

For consciousness, single-iterative electrical frequencies are not contiguous. Each ingressing single-iterative frequency is infinitesimally harmonized at egress for favorable fitment for the next corresponding neuron. Input-thru-output is harmonized and "re-frequencied" at egress as a reformed *unique electrical signature key*. Re-frequencied unique electrical signature key defaults only to the closest majorly similar neuron whose ingress frequency majorly matches the re-frequenced single-iterative output of the preceding neuron. Essentially, the lineage for and from primordial-consciousness.

The neurotubule structure's alternating polarity defaultively re-harmonizes ingressing frequency for the electrical output to seek acceptance by a sequentially-receptive neuron. For example, the output from neuron "An" ("n" = number) is re-harmonized to sequence to the next neuron, not necessarily "Bn". It can be "An" to "Cn," or "Fn," and so on–not linear but proximate-closest *both* physically and electrically. Example: neuron Bn that accepts from An biologically inputs An's electrical tolerance only if harmonized frequency "mostly fits" Bn input polarity. The resultant unique electrical signature key unlocks the next neuron "door." The output frequency is passively tuned, coursing through each neurotubule, but not deliberately so; it is entirely by biological default, a result of boolean functional reconciliation due to the leisure of evolution. Greater neurotubule activities strengthen areas into "neuronicalities": Dendrite-neurotransmitter-synapse.

> *Consciousness is the introspective objectification of empathetic sophistication.*

Consciousness is the primary construction governing the emotional, psychological, and logical function of each specie's iterative/individual. Logic exists first as it's a fundamental mathematical basis of life and reflects basic biological choices and behavior; boolean biological mathematic provides spherical physical directions (dendrite construction), allowing for physical compartmentalization of falsepositives. Logic processing evolved from a random option into a standard design, such as stochastic trait popularity by volume.

Moderate-, complex-, and sophisticated-consciousnesses' emotive constructions are secondly caused, while psychological comprisement structure is third, albeit wholesale manifested. Evolution subsists entirely upon iterative reconcile/confirm; pre-Darwin and thereafter. Darwinism's "survival" mandate essentially is the sophistication of consciousness in its reconciliation and confirmation processing structure (generational).

Referencing LUCA[70]–the Last Universal Common Ancestor–consciousness ultimately derives from the natural schematics of *first cells*. Evolution defaulted by compartmentalizing falsepositives as a reconciliatory biological-mathematical exhaust due to irrationality of subdecimal infinity being logically computable and thus compartmentalized biologically. Otherwise,

---

[70] https://en.wikipedia.org/wiki/Last_universal_common_ancestor

Darwinism couldn't hold true—phylogenetic point-of-foundate for species' consciousnesses. Consciousness of species divaricates, emerges due from evolutional time-scale sophistication of neuronality; it has evolved heredity into functionally self-aware biological structures (species), furthering its diversification into all evolution: the psychogenesis of consciousness.

The failed comprehension of consciousness is due to remarkable human hubris: "I'm unique from all other species." Academia, spiritualists, and religious mantras, whose historically uniform message has a virulently insecure habit of claiming that "humans are special." Human self-questioning arrogance that a "deliberate" demarcation of sophisticated consciousness must be a human-exclusive benefit or award. Lauded opines would be laughed at by any advanced-consciousness foreign-planet alien specie(s) within our universe. It very much reflects the human-specie's uncouth "consciousness" for ideating fantastical suppositions of its consciousness via systems—which literally anthropomorphizes conjectures of human existence as unique. The fault lies in failing to recognize the seemingly infinite, gossamer-thin evolutionary steps necessary for the construction of consciousness and in failing to scale consciousness beyond human-specie idiomaticity.

The uniqueness of consciousness isn't unique.

Life is not a right under the law of evolution. Separating "life" from "consciousness" is a miscomprehension. Evolution aggregates entireness despite the fact that current human-specie are not all at the same stage of evolutionary development. The human-specie's conceit mollified predation into coherent familial sociality through an understanding of safety and protection within a family-group and the reconciliatory default of evolution to construct intra- and co-dependencies (familial sociality evolution as emotively familial isomorphism). Biology and logic dictate that familial-species closely relate to one another and shall share similar schematic consciousness expressions, with varying psychosomatic manifestations within each taxon's homogeneous construction. Consciousness at the corresponding dilutive scale evokes stereotypic psychosomatic manifestations due to emotive-isomorphism quantification.

Early consciousness follows simple evolutionary paths: primordial-consciousness, primal-consciousness, intro-consciousness, simple-consciousness, moderate-consciousness, and sophisticated-consciousnesses. Consciousness is mathematically plottable biology.

Briefly: Arf Arf Bark Bark Theorem and Its Why

Had I pursued an academic career in law or psychology, I would have been stuck in a rigid linear perspective. Were physics my pursuit, I would never consider "irrationality" the primary nature of mathematic. Had I pursued zoology, behaviorism, or "dog training," I would have been taught that all dangerous dogs and animals must be killed due to the hopelessness of academia. My profound intelligence would have been stifled and wasted. Professors would have vehemently instructed me that dysfunctional dogs like Gordon, Axel, MiQi the Golden Retriever,[71] Walter, and Hugo were categorically "impossible" to be familially integrated or socially cogent at home and in public. Behaviorism conveniently declaring "death as the only hope."

Being the first person in human history to quantify and comprehend the phylogenesis of consciousness, my book is a warning of the irrevocable, limited existence of humanity. The human-specie is evolutionally diverging into two distinct taxa, of which its majorly extinction is unavoidable. Materialist-predation that once aggregated human sophisticated consciousness beneficially for centuries, now careens extinctive. Materialist-predation humans comprising the lower-boolean taxon will succeed predominantly again, but instead of a socially-functional revolution, this second occurrence shall result in human-specie eradication. It is impossible to devolve the behavior of those who control the world, much less societally or cognitively influence eight billion people evolutionally. Climate change is specious; stochastically the human-specie will simply migrate inland or to habitable regions currently uncivilized, requiring as few as twenty thousand individuals to sustain its specie regardless of attriting eight billion. Major self-extinction will occur within four hundred years (twenty generations) due to the next two materialist-predation fueled world wars. Despite human-specie's brag of adaptability, such as for grand technology, removing its behavior inter alia consciousness is evolutionally impossible. Consider history's guide; it has been less than one hundred years (five generations) since the first two world wars.[72] Behavior is *nature <u>and</u> nurture*.

Artificial intelligence won't "destroy humanity"; if so, it will always be due to anthropomorphic programming. This misguidance is as old as human

---

[71] Arf Arf Bark Bark Rescue & Rehab, "Mickey the Golden - Single Session - Day 1 (James) and Day 2 with his foster (R. W.)," *YouTube*, posted January 7, 2023, https://www.youtube.com/watch?app=desktop&v=Dy3BuqDbcfE

[72] https://en.wikipedia.org/wiki/World_war

conceit. Artificial intelligence exists without a timescale, hence no urgency to motivate materialist-predation. It won't be "artificial intelligence" that extinguishes the burning candle of humanity.

Caution to wholesale plunge headfirst in the belief of achieving artificial consciousness (Artificial General Intelligence, Artificial Super Intelligence, "gentle singularity"), it's akin to following the wrong GPS directions. In fact, the current programming-technology infrastructure is, at best, a simplistic template plagiarizing the theory of quantum computing, obfuscated by immodest human hubristic semantic and anthropomorphic naivety. For example, biological intelligence human brains utilize the same finite biological constructional operation. Anomalies of intelligence within the human-specie are random stochastic popularity–without additional power, memory, or processing chips. Intelligence variation is due to degrees of sophisticated introvertive idiomatic contextualization relative to each individual's wholesale objectification, environment, ecology, and *nurture* conforming to evolutional default.

> *The fact is that the human brain has a finite size. The brain's processing power doesn't get "added on" with extra Blackwell chips or more gigawatts of power. My brain is roughly the same as every other adult. I'm not using more power, either. The reason why I comprehend more is because I am idiomatically contextualizing a larger swath of information despite still using roughly the same amount of brain power. Case in point is that I have a grade 10 education, yet I'm connecting all the information I've read and learned and applying logic to reconcile. Same human brain.*
>
> *(My email to Marinel Balde, HR and Operations Lead, Leaders Press)*

My comprehension of consciousness provides me with a unique interpretation of evolution. Artificial consciousness can't be achieved or correctly built without adhering to the same evolutional construction structure for biological consciousness. AI, AGI, and SI are "Electronic Simulated Intelligence." The apropos of artificial intelligence is not postulating demarcate of superior general aptitude,[73] but for its computational concurrence of the universe's mathematic formulaic spanning from pre-Singularity to biological consciousness to Artificial Contextual Intelligence

[73] https://tinyurl.com/ydusbb53

and possibly the penultimate evolution of hybridization (thus creating a new specie as if peer to God).

Current artificial intelligence is unable to mechanically generate or compartmentalize the irrationality of falsepositive output. Genuine artificial consciousness shall idiomatically contextualize historical relevance through "best conflation practices" mathematic. The reliance upon volumic token parameters of massive brute force mirrors pseudo-quantum computing pyramidically. Congruency mandates that artificial consciousness capably literate the actual phylogenetic construction of biological consciousness in written formulaic and articulate comprehensibly to all levels of people and articulably quantify psychosomatic manifestations among all species. Artificial consciousness must be able to describe thyself, and the sequence of the universe. My capacity to empirically comprehend all psychosomatic manifestations relies on the efficiency of my non-modular, relatively limited intelligence. I've discussed with Leaders Press the technological advancement in the YouTube video *"HUGE Breakthrough In Computing with Light"* as at four percent toward correctly designing Artificial Contextual Intelligence.[74]

To reconcile my theorem into a simple formulaic, I delved toward the construction of the universe and why its malleability of mathematic permitted the biological construct of consciousness toward sophisticated existence here and on similar planets. A mathematic permitting any singularity to exist obligates that an equilibrium with its containment, such as a "supervacuum," is conducive to sudden inflation rather than an inert or impotent dispersal. Before the universe, *time* existed pre-singularity, existing in both motion and motionless without measure unto a single axis. As a child, I opined to my dad: that time is an omni-dimensional viscosity and that time and mathematic are inconvertible and immanent omni-dimensions across all universes; real, theorized, and imagined—God itself is not the creator of, yet is beholden and bound with time and mathematic.

It's very important that God is not anthropomorphized nor painted through pareidolia as being specific gender nor lent to nor affine as a certain specie. God is of no gender nor specie nor embodiment. Albeit "it" reflects my abhor of calling dogs "it" and when conversing about animals due to biological genders. Despite hurting religious feelings, defining God as "it" is logical despite the human incessant to anthropomorphize omnipotence and

---

[74] Anastashi In Tech, "Why Light Will Change Everything," *YouTube*, posted August 22, 2025, https://www.youtube.com/watch?v=b_PS8o8pi9A

omniscience. Ironic inanity for theological debate to "insult" by objectifying God as an inanimate by removing gender of the Creator for what is not a biological existence.

I proposed to my dad that within mathematic are three complexities of quantum physics: **Super Quantum Physics** (re: supervacuum), **Superior Quantum Physics** (the catalyzation of the singularity into separation as disaggregate matter, or "quantum composition value"), and the current **Inferior Quantum Physics** (post-singularity). No singularity can inflate without movement, requiring either divine deliberacy or infrastructural failure from an initial catalyst. An initial catalyst indicates measure and movement within the singularity's motionless.

It seemed nonsensical to seek immensely complex theories without bearing logic that all mathematic formulas, regardless of complexity, always adhere to the basics of quantification. Regardless of universe, multi-universes, or theorized universes, the quantity of "one" is still "one" in all universes, real and imagined. Mathematic will function exactly the same. Like the singularity, quantity begins at "one."

"Quantum composition value" relies on the first three simple logic expressions simultaneously, which rely on the three complexities of quantum physics, at the singularity's first point of disaggregation: the "first piece of matter or energy" separating from the singularity:

$$1 + 1$$

$$1 - 1$$

$$1 \text{ and } 1$$

The irrefutable first three simultaneous mathematic rules for every universe*. This led me to consider the universe didn't occur via the euphemistic "Big Bang" but rather a Big Friction due to the initiating catalyst infrastructurally failing sequentially in nature and determining its non-spheric shape. Though inflation exceeded the speed of light, it contended against the nominal resistance of the supervacuum experiencing blowback-and-friction, and against its exterior edge of expansion cooling and reabsorbed into its inflation.

---

* *The physical theory for "why 2+2?" Why Does 2 + 2 = 4? What Math Teaches Us About Deep Reality https://www.youtube.com/watch?v=bY3ZMOn9mHQ*

Cyclic universes are implausible due to attrition of matter and energy, preventing "Big Crunch" from occurring as the amount of matter attrited from the original content required of the "first" singularity. A second "Big Bang" would not have had sufficient mass for superior quantum physics to catalyze it to "singularity." For example, the cosmic microwave background[75] will have travelled far beyond gravity and contraction–the tangible mathematical quantity of lost subdecimal infinity values.

Fast-forward: consciousness evolved due to aggregative conflation inherent in biological mathematical malleability, the ability to compartmentalize irrationality in the bottom-half of each subdecimal infinity number. Hence, consciousness' formulaic:

$$C = (<1 \text{ and } >0)$$

The attainment of true artificial consciousness intelligence obligates functionality to mechanically compartmentalize finitely-infinite falsepositives. The good news is that it's not a daunting technological proposal. I know my empirical comprehension of behavior and consciousness is unique and commercially proprietary. It unsubstantiates and injures artificial intelligence neurology and its lauded authorities. *The Soul of a Dog* provides both the phylogenesis and psychogenesis of consciousness. I see several newer technologies currently in existence/experimentation that, when collectively integrated, will physically compartmentalize falsepostive output: genuine artificial consciousness akin to biological consciousness. Artificial contextual intelligence will develop quasi-quantum computers. And engineers will eventually start building '*human-safe robots*' for consumers.

To close, the *Arf Arf Bark Bark Theorem of Consciousness and of Learning* is not whimsically-named. It's titled to be a constant tribute and reminder for the lives of those who were so ineptly miscomprehended that they were all needlessly killed through *behavioral euthanasia*. Within this theorem is the very strong inference for preventing human-specie self-extinction. Its writing is based on its uniform empirical success. It is teachable and learnable for all levels and types of dedicated parents because its anthropomorphic intuitive simplicity exceedingly surpasses behaviorism academia.

Behavior is psychological. Not hungry.

---

[75] https://en.wikipedia.org/wiki/Cosmic_microwave_background

www.ingramcontent.com/pod-product-compliance
Lightning Source LLC
Chambersburg PA
CBHW051447050726
47593CB00005B/1963

* 9 7 8 1 6 3 7 3 5 2 7 6 2 *